Born and bred in Liverpool, Sue moved to the Loughborough University and thereafter continue conference and events' organiser and subsequently company. Following a period at home bringing up her children, she began work as a special needs assistant, working over the next few years in two local primary schools. She also gained a Post-Graduate Diploma in drama therapy at the Roehampton Institute and enjoyed a stint as a school governor. Sue has been involved for many years in running after-school drama clubs and workshops and has helped to devise and run several holiday clubs. She has published a book of sketches and stories for churches and schools, entitled Brush Strokes (Kevin Mayhew, 2004) and also works with popular songwriters Mark and Helen Johnson and Margaret Carpenter. Sue has written the scripts for ten 'Out of the Ark Music' productions, including Stable Manners, Hoodwinked, Wind in the Willows and, most recently, Cinderella 'n' Rockerfella.

Sue has also been involved for many years with a church-based drama group, Vision Theatre, writing scripts, performing and operating puppets. She is currently attempting to develop ventriloquism skills and, in her spare time, is an accomplished liar, acting at Murder Mystery dinners for a company called The Killing Game. Beware!

Sue now lives in Surrey with her husband, Paul. They have two grown-up children and four dogs.

Barnabas
for
Children®

Barnabas for Children® is a registered word mark and the logo is a registered device mark of The Bible Reading Fellowship.

Text copyright © Sue Langwade 2013
Illustrations copyright © Mark Brierley 2013
The author asserts the moral right
to be identified as the author of this work

Published by
The Bible Reading Fellowship
15 The Chambers, Vineyard
Abingdon OX14 3FE
United Kingdom
Tel: +44 (0)1865 319700
Email: enquiries@brf.org.uk
Website: www.brf.org.uk
BRF is a Registered Charity

ISBN 978 1 84101 884 3
First published 2013
10 9 8 7 6 5 4 3 2 1 0
All rights reserved

Acknowledgments
Unless otherwise stated, scripture quotations are taken from the Contemporary English Version of the Bible published by HarperCollins Publishers, copyright © 1991, 1992, 1995 American Bible Society.

Scripture quotations taken from the Holy Bible, New International Version, copyright © 1973, 1978, 1984 by International Bible Society, are used by permission of Hodder & Stoughton Publishers, a member of the Hachette Livre Group UK. All rights reserved. 'NIV' is a registered trademark of International Bible Society. UK trademark number 1448790.

Scriptures quoted from the Good News Bible published by The Bible Societies/HarperCollins Publishers Ltd, UK © American Bible Society 1966, 1971, 1976, 1992, used with permission.

The paper used in the production of this publication was supplied by mills that source their raw materials from sustainably managed forests. Soy-based inks were used in its printing and the laminate film is biodegradable.

A catalogue record for this book is available from the British Library

Printed in Singapore by Craft Print International Ltd

Let's Get Together!

Flexible fun-filled activity ideas
for the whole church family

Sue Langwade

This book is dedicated to my mum, Eileen, now rejoicing in heaven, and to my dad, John, and sister, Pat, with heartfelt thanks for showing me what family is all about.

Acknowledgments

Huge thanks to all those who have supported and encouraged me in the writing of this book and the trialling of the material, particularly the Messy Church team at Walton Baptist church: Lizette, Ruth, Sue H, Beryl, Dorothy, Linda, Yvonne, Miriam, Susie and Sam. Lots of love to Mark and Helen Johnson, whose encouragement by text was often so timely!

A rousing round of applause to Vision Theatre regulars, Pat, Rob, Phil and Diana, and supporters: the other Sue, Judy, Sam, Amber and Rainier, who made doing the dramas such fun.

A special thank you must go to my dear friend, Jane Sachdev, who has been amazingly generous with her time and many giftings. She has listened, pondered, advised and fed me cake—what a gem! And to the amazing Jenny Hamill, who also fed me royally and made me laugh!

I have been extremely blessed in receiving invaluable advice and delicious tea from Stewart and Carol Henderson and Margaret and Steven Cox, and in being surrounded by my beautiful daughters and ever-patient husband. I would like to thank my dogs for their advice on the character of Chip and for keeping me sane by making me pick up the lead and walk. And last, but definitely not least, a debt of gratitude is owed to Joan and the area six housegroup who have prayed, and to Sue Doggett, who has patiently guided me through the development of this project with grace and wisdom.

With thanks to Paul Langwade for all the original music (see www.barnabasinchurches.org.uk/extra-resources/).

Contents

Introduction

One surefire way of building strong relationships is to have fun together—and if that fun involves learning something about our heavenly Father along the way, all the better. The material in this book is intended to provide opportunities to do just that in a variety of ways. Included are five themed sessions, each one using craft, storytelling, games and challenges, puppets, a serial drama, an interactive sketch and a reflective prayer time to explore an aspect of the umbrella theme for the five sessions, which is 'family' (explored through the metaphor of a tree). The focus for the individual sessions is as follows:

1. Belonging (the tree is planted)
2. Appropriate boundaries and encouragement (the sapling tree)
3. Valuing ourselves and others (the tree bears fruit)
4. Sharing what we have (the tree sends out seeds)
5. Resting on God's promises (the tree in maturity)

Each session lasts approximately two hours, although it could be shortened by omitting some of the elements or lengthened by adding in a time for refreshments. The sessions can be linked to provide a consecutive five-day programme, culminating in an optional family-friendly service; they can be delivered individually over a longer time-frame, or each session can stand alone as a 'one-off'. (You will find a prospective timetable for a full session on page 9.) Alternatively, the various elements that make up the sessions can be used independently, providing you with a flexible resource for use in a wide range of contexts such as inclusive, family-friendly acts of worship, church weekends away, churches working together initiatives and so on.

For example, you might use one of the stories to complement or introduce a short talk. Although the stories are linked to a session theme, the content is broad-based enough to allow for other applications, the subjects of the stories being:

• The names and character of God
• The Ten Commandments

- The value of all gifting
- The feeding of the five thousand
- Trusting God as our heavenly Father

Likewise, the serial drama and puppet sketches can be used to introduce key words or themes in a humorous way, as it is often valuable to start with a light-hearted approach before you dig a little deeper. As we see in the proverb below, laughter is good for us and promotes a positive outlook, so humour can be a powerful tool in helping to get your point across. You will find key words printed at the beginning of the scripts for both the drama and puppet sketches.

If you are cheerful, you feel good; if you are sad, you hurt all over.
PROVERBS 17:22

Furthermore, as people usually enjoy meeting familiar characters in a drama or puppet sketch, you might like to present this material as an episodic series, weekly or monthly, using the 'Bible bloodhound' resource as a follow-up. This suggests activities to be done at home, which reinforce the themes and link them to Bible verses.

Also, if you have a particularly keen drama team, they may like to present all five episodes of the drama as part of an evening's family entertainment.

The crafts, challenges and reflective prayer ideas are all suitable for inclusion in any family-friendly event and, as the actions for the interactive sketch can be taught quite quickly in one session, it could be used in any situation where you want a creative way to emphasise the love of God for all his children.

However you choose to use the material, the idea is for the whole church family to draw together to participate in any or all of the above-mentioned, time-tested family activities and, in the process, to develop and deepen relationships, both with one another and with God. The object is to encourage people of all ages to chill out and laugh together while being prompted to think and chat about this wonderful God and about faith and family issues in a relaxed environment. As it is intended that the exploration and discovery should continue at home, the approach is one of seed-sowing rather than in-depth teaching, which can be undertaken in more age-appropriate settings at another time. The activities suggested should get people's attention; the response is up to them. As Matthew 11:15 points out, we need to choose to use our ears: 'If you have ears, pay attention!'

Should you choose to run one or more full sessions, the following timetable provides an example of how the session could be organised. This should keep the pace fairly rapid and give a reasonable mix of static and non-static activities (space and numbers allowing, of course).

Registration/Welcome activities (including 'Quick craft')	15–20 minutes	Various
Starter activity/housekeeping	10 minutes	All together
Puppet sketch	10 minutes	All together
Team challenge	15–20 minutes	In groups
Story	10 minutes	All together
Craft	15–20 minutes	In groups
Interactive sketch	10 minutes	All together
Serial drama	10 minutes	All together
Sharing/Reflective prayer	15 minutes	In groups

NB: The team challenge and crafts could run simultaneously, as long as you keep strictly to time.

Tree dwelling

Why a tree theme? First of all, the words 'family' and 'tree' are already usefully connected in the human consciousness. As we read in Genesis 1:11, trees come in a wide variety, just like families. It is good to note that we have a God who likes diversity in his creation: 'God said, "I command the earth to produce all kinds of plants, including fruit trees and grain." And that's what happened' (Genesis 1:11).

Just as there are many types of trees of all shapes and sizes, with each type having unique qualities, so each expression of 'family' is made up of a collection of individuals, whether we're talking about nuclear family, church family or global family, and is therefore going to be unlike any other. However, just as all trees have certain requirements that need to be met in order for them to thrive, so it is with these various family structures. There are certain godly principles that might apply on a small scale to our day-to-day family, and on a large scale in the broader sense of the word. As we ponder some of those things that all trees have in common (namely roots, shoots and fruits), we might consider what are some of the roots—or foundational principles—that can help our families to develop in a wholesome way.

When these roots are firmly established, the shoots and fruits should be a natural outcome. For example, when we know that we belong, we have a sense of identity and security (the tree is planted); when appropriate boundaries are in place and are enforced, along with much encouragement, the result should be the development of a good conscience, healthy self-esteem and so on (the sapling tree); when we learn to be content with who we are and to value both ourselves and others, we can gain fulfilment in using our strengths and learning from the challenges of working together with others whose strengths complement our own (the tree bears fruit); when we are willing to share both who we are and what we have, we can see the divine principle of multiplication at work (the tree sends out seeds); and when we trust God as our heavenly Father, we can relax and enjoy a blossoming relationship with him (the tree in maturity).

Just like trees, families have seasons, both in terms of the various life experiences they encounter and the organic growth that takes place as individuals attempt to learn to live together in harmony. If the root system is strong enough, in a natural sense in trees and in a figurative one in families, both can withstand most difficulties.

Trees need to be planted in a suitable environment, in good mineral-rich soil, with access to adequate food, water, light and air. In the same way, our families need to be rooted and grounded in love and fed good nutritional fare, whether in a physical or spiritual sense. There are obvious connections in this way to several biblical allegories: God's word as the seed sown on good soil; Jesus as the bread of life and the living water; the Holy Spirit as wind (moving air). In summary, a healthy, fruitful family is one that has its roots firmly established in God's word, feeds on Jesus and is sensitive to the breeze of the Holy Spirit.

The tree metaphor follows a progressive route, looking at a different aspect of 'tree life' in each session. It therefore lends itself to an ongoing visual representation. This could take the form of a two-dimensional display or a more elaborate three-dimensional one, depending on the resources you have available (of this, more later).

As mentioned earlier, there are five stages, each explored in one of the five sessions.

- The tree is planted (belonging)
- The sapling tree (appropriate boundaries and encouragement)
- The tree bears fruit (valuing ourselves and others)
- The tree sends out seeds (sharing what we have)
- The tree in maturity (resting on God's promises)

Session One: The tree is planted

Theme: Belonging

Tree link

Just as trees are planted, so we are planted by God. We are not accidental: we belong on his family tree.

Bible link

He came into his own world, but his own nation did not welcome him. Yet some people accepted him and put their faith in him. So he gave them the right to be the children of God. They were not God's children by nature or because of any human desires. God himself was the one who made them his children.

JOHN 1:11–13

Belonging is a recognised basic human need—not surprisingly, as God made us to belong, in terms of community and family. In fact, as God is an utterly unified Trinity, belonging is also a quintessential part of the divine make-up. We can belong to earthly families, to spiritual families and to a global family. When we belong to God's family, his nature becomes part of us (2 Peter 1:4); when we really take on board the magnificence and privilege of being one of God's children, our sense of identity is transformed, no longer based on the expectations and say-so of a fallen world, but on the acceptance, affirmation and unconditional love lavished on us by a God who chooses to call himself our daddy (Abba). Wow! As our heavenly Father, God undertakes to watch over us and provide for all our needs.

Perhaps 'belonging' brings with it a sense of responsibility, as 'we are each part of the body of Christ, as well as part of one another' (Romans 12:5). So we see 'family' extending beyond those with whom we share our household and possibly blood ties, to those with whom we worship, as well as the many, worldwide, with whom we share our faith in Christ. It is good to consider what responsibility we have to these people also and what we can do to discharge that responsibility, perhaps praying, working together and sharing resources.

As individuals, we often like to meet with others who share similar interests. When we choose to belong to clubs and societies, we find out something about them, making sure that they are suitable for us. Likewise, it is good to find out about the God to whom we belong, especially as we are made in his image. One of the ways in which God has chosen to reveal his character is through his names. This fact has been used as the focus of the story in Session One, by offering a whistle-stop tour through just a few of God's names. With this in mind, you might like to have some others displayed or arrange a time to look at his names in greater detail (see page 124).

Overview of the session

Quick craft	Add your handprint to God's family tree (p. 38)
Starter activity	Making un-separateable squash (p. 34)
Puppet sketch	George finds something in his carrot patch that doesn't belong there (p. 76)
Team challenge	Matching pairs; Belonga conga (pp. 50–51)
Story	The names of God (p. 59)
Crafts	The bunting of belonging; name jewellery (pp. 39–40)
Serial drama	The Wood family adopt a rather special dog (p. 88)
Reflective prayer	Your name is written on the palm of God's hand (p. 113)

Session Two: The sapling tree
Theme: Appropriate boundaries and encouragement

Tree link

Until trees are well established, they benefit from some form of protection, such as a translucent wrap placed around the base of the tree to protect it from the effects of harsh weather, pets, wild animals, strimmers and chemical sprays—

anything that might damage it. This does not hinder the growth of the tree but simply helps to keep it free from harm. In the same way, God has provided us with guidance that will assist us to lead healthy, fulfilling lives and will help to keep us safe from things that would damage us and corrode our relationship with him.

Bible link

Teach your children right from wrong, and when they are grown they will still do right.
PROVERBS 22:6

It is important for a young tree to receive the right nourishment, just as we need to be sure to nourish one another with encouraging words. In the letter to the church in Ephesus, we read, 'Say the right thing at the right time and help others by what you say' (Ephesians 4:29).

Discipline, as in the applying of certain rules and strictures, is cited in the Bible as being something positive, a necessary means of keeping us in check. It is a service that parents or people in authority can provide for those under their care, to encourage them to make good choices and develop a healthy conscience. However, an overly authoritarian discipline is not a reflection of the way in which God deals with us, his children. His discipline is consistent, fair and accompanied by a great deal of encouragement and affirmation. It is all too easy within our earthly families to allow familiarity to breed contempt and to forget that our family members are as deserving of a gracious response from us as outsiders are.

Appropriate boundaries and encouragement are like two sides of one coin, working together to produce a well-balanced person or a well-ordered community (as the institutions with which we are concerned—family, church and global communities—are all relational).

In the Old Testament, God gave the Israelites the Ten Commandments and, as Jesus came to fulfil the law and not to abolish it, we can assume that these Commandments still have relevance for us today. They provide the basis for the story that features in Session Two, with a little artistic licence having been used to try to capture the heart behind them—to foster an understanding that God's rules are not intended to restrict us unnecessarily but to bring clarity and a sense of order.

The tendency to deny any absolutes has the effect of painting God, who has given us some quite definite advice on how to live, as an outmoded, despotic jobsworth. To think like that is to misunderstand the heart of God, whose desire is always for our well-being. He is not some archaic schoolteacher poring over our mistakes, red pen hovering, with a mean glint in his eye. His guidance comes hand-in-hand with grace. Thankfully, he values our jerky, erratic attempts as we learn to dance to the rhythm of his heartbeat. He loves our faltering steps in the right direction. He would plead for us not to 'put our hand in the fire' not because he wants to deny us the right to experience having our flesh burnt, but because he knows it will hurt like mad and could cause long-term damage.

The most important thing when 'laying down the law', as we do sometimes have to do in all the expressions of family, is to be sure that there is a loving motivation and that a huge hug, a word of praise and a forgiving heart are always ready and waiting on the sidelines—hence the juxtaposition in the programme of boundaries and encouragement. This is demonstrated in the words of 1 Corinthians 13:4–8:

Love is kind and patient, never jealous, boastful, proud, or rude. Love isn't selfish or quick-tempered. It doesn't keep a record of wrongs that others do. Love rejoices in the truth, but not in evil. Love is always supportive, loyal, hopeful, and trusting. Love never fails!

Overview of the session

Quick craft	Make bricks to build a clay wall (p. 41)
Starter activity	Silly laws quiz (pp. 35, 122)
Puppet sketch	George tries his hand at fencing (p. 78)
Team challenge	Obstacle course; marble run (pp. 51–52)
Story	The Ten Commandments (p. 63)
Crafts	Commandment hangings; pompoms of encouragement (pp. 41–42)
Serial drama	The Wood family train Chip. Or do they? (p. 92)
Reflective prayer	The two most important commandments (p. 114)

Session Three: The tree bears fruit
Theme: Valuing ourselves and others

Tree link

All trees that are classed as 'flowering plants' bear fruit. There is a wide variety, allowing for different climatic conditions and divergent tastes. I'm so glad God is a God of variety. It might be wonderful to see a 'host of golden daffodils', but it's even better when, a few months later, you might encounter a field of lilac lavender or a gathering of perky poppies. The spice of life, indeed!

Bible link

You did not choose me. I chose you and sent you out to produce fruit, the kind of fruit that will last. Then my Father will give you whatever you ask for in my name. So I command you to love each other.
JOHN 15:16–17

Bearing fruit is a natural progression in the life of trees. They cannot make themselves bear fruit or, indeed, choose the fruit that they will bear. Given the right conditions, they will automatically produce fruit according to their kind. They don't look at one another and compare themselves, unfavourably or otherwise (at least, not in the real world!). They fulfil the purpose for which they were intended.

Likewise, God has instilled within each of us 'fruit' of some sort—a gifting; an ability that is to be used to benefit others. As we each allow our fruit to develop and to be part of the great fruit salad of family (earthly, church and global community), we can enjoy the sense of being useful and of working together with others, being respected and learning to respect those who are different from us. In Galatians 6:4–5 we read, 'Do your own work well, and then you will have something to be proud of. But don't compare yourself with others. We each must carry our own load.'

Just as we all have the potential to bear fruit of one kind or another, we also all have the potential to prefer the fruit of others to the fruit that God has ordained us to produce: the grass is always greener on the other side of the fence. It is a fairly well-established fact that true happiness lies in being content with what we have. When we compare ourselves with others, it rarely has a helpful outcome.

The usual consequence is that we develop either a sense of inferiority or a wrong sort of pride. We need to believe that we are individually valuable and not be threatened by those we perceive to be more gifted than we are. It helps if we can ensure that all gifts are equally valued—that we avoid a hierarchy of gifts, confusing function and status. God considers us all utterly precious, regardless of what we can or cannot do.

The story in Session Three focuses on seeds that are initially disgruntled because they feel that they do all the right things but do not become what they wanted to be. It takes the wisdom of a mature tree to explain to them that true happiness lies in being content with what you are.

Other aspects of the programme look at what can be achieved when we work together and appreciate what others have to offer, thus functioning as a healthy body. Within our families, it can be difficult to develop the habit of appreciating the different tastes in food, music, clothes and so on. While there is obviously a need for parents and carers to bring wisdom to bear in these areas, it is useful to discern the difference between personal preferences and godly direction. I have to ask myself from time to time, is it perhaps too coincidental that God happens to like the same radio stations, clothing stores and films as I do?

Overview of the session

Quick craft	Make a plant pot and plant a bulb (p. 43)
Starter activity	Charades (p. 35)
Puppet sketch	George tries to buy a fruit salad tree (p. 80)
Team challenge	Moving fruit; fruit salad plus (pp. 52–53)
Story	The song of the seeds (p. 66)
Crafts	Windmills; seed mosaic (p. 44)
Serial drama	The Wood family work together to build a kennel for Chip (p. 95)
Reflective prayer	Sharing fruit (p. 114)

Session Four: The tree sends out seeds
Theme: Sharing what we have

Tree link

Every tree carries within itself seeds that can be sent out in order to reproduce more trees. It's an everyday miracle, really. It is amazing to realise that a sturdy, regal oak began life as an acorn, and yet this is a principle that we see at work time and time again within the topsy-turvy kingdom of God: the small things are not despised; the least is the greatest; multitudes are fed from a small boy's lunch. God gives us blessings so that we can 'pay them forward' and bless others. In kingdom terms, multiplication is the name of the game.

Bible link

Jesus looked up and saw some rich people tossing their gifts into the offering box. He also saw a poor widow putting in two pennies. And he said, 'I tell you that this poor woman has put in more than all the others. Everyone else gave what they didn't need. But she is very poor and gave everything she had.'

LUKE 21:1–4

This session focuses on giving what we have, back to God, in order that he can multiply it, as only he can do. The session is also about giving to others. This type of giving can include a smile, a word of encouragement, finance, resources, time, mentoring or role-modelling. And there's nothing so small or seemingly insignificant that God can't use it. Splendid!

We are asked to give as freely as we have received (Matthew 10:8b). We are not given goods, gifts and so on to hang on to them or let them rot. As every tree reproduces itself, so we are encouraged to mentor others, share what we have, provide good role models and be spiritual parents. God is not limited by the amount we have to offer, only by the attitude in which the offering is made. The fantastic thing is that our giving can have a ripple effect, sometimes achieving far more than we could have anticipated.

The story in Session Four is based on the feeding of the five thousand, an event in which the miracle of divine multiplication can clearly be seen at work. What I find fascinating about this story is that, while I am convinced that God is a master mathematician and could no doubt have calculated how much food would be needed to the nearest crumb, yet we see twelve basketsful left over. What a wonderful picture of his abundant, overflowing giving! It also makes me feel much better about my complete inability to calculate the amount of spaghetti needed to feed a family of four. Those are days when the dogs eat well.

There is a film called *Pay It Forward*, based on a book of the same name by Catherine Ryan Hyde, in which a young boy has the idea that the world could be changed by repaying any good deed 'forward'—that is by doing three good deeds to others to 'repay' the one from which he has benefited. It is an interesting notion and one that we could do worse than to adopt, provided our focus remains on what God can do through us, not on our own goodness. If anyone in your group has the DVD, it would be an interesting one to make available for borrowing.

Overview of the session

Quick craft	Ice some biscuits or cakes (p. 45)
Starter activity	Pass it on! (p. 36)
Puppet sketch	Multiplying marrows (p. 88)
Team challenge	Balloon-blow football; making shapes (p. 54)
Story	The feeding of the five thousand (p. 69)
Crafts	Family photo tree; rockin' person award (pp. 46–47)
Serial drama	Chip sacrifices his best bone to cheer up the Wood family (p. 99)
Reflective prayer	Stones and ripples (p. 115)

Session Five: The tree in maturity
Theme: Resting on God's promises

Tree link

There is something rather majestic about a mature tree. It provides shelter and shade, as well as being a thing of beauty. As noted in the Bible link below, it can withstand almost anything. A similar idea is expressed in the parable of the house built on the rock, but somehow the picture of something living and thriving and ongoing, after the frailty of its early years, is even more awe-inspiring. To aspire to that same sense of sure strength, all we have to do is trust in God. It's sometimes easier said than done, of course, but we will never have that certainty until we send out *our* roots (often in great trepidation, it must be said), only to find that they are indeed immersed in the source of life.

Bible link

I will bless those who trust me. They will be like trees growing beside a stream—trees with roots that reach down to the water, and with leaves that are always green. They will bear fruit every year and are never worried by a lack of rain.

JEREMIAH 17:7–8

God encourages us to shelter in him and trust in his ability to help us withstand any storm that might come our way. Even when we fall, underneath us are the everlasting arms (Deuteronomy 33:27, NIV). Therefore, we can know freedom from worry and fear, despite circumstances, because he has promised to be always 'watching our backs' (see Psalm 121), and he always keeps his promises.

No surprise, then, that in Session Five our focus is on trusting God and celebrating the fact that he keeps his promises. There should be a party atmosphere as we relax into the freedom that comes from knowing that the gospel is one of grace, that God is our trustworthy daddy (the theme of the story), and that there are promises to claim for our families, in the assurance that God will honour them. This seems a suitable cause for celebration! Furthermore, when we take time to relax and have fun together, bonds are forged and deepened.

Overview of the session

Quick craft	Balloon names (p. 47)
Starter activity	Messy eating (p. 37)
Puppet sketch	George and Ted shelter from the storm (p. 84)
Team challenge	The chocolate game; beat the goalie (p. 55)
Story	Trusting God as our dad (p. 72)

Crafts	Balloon party plates; promise boxes (pp. 48–49)
Serial drama	Teresa is rescued by Aquaman (p. 102)
Reflective prayer	Rainbow promises (p. 115)

Chat time

In this section you will find some Bible verses, some points for consideration and some questions for discussion, all relating to the session themes. These verses could be used personally or as a team, before your event, to help clarify your thinking on the themes. Alternatively, you might like to meditate on one or more of the verses and then use the statements and questions to begin to explore them. They are by no means exhaustive but are a useful starting point.

Session One

Theme: Belonging

Helpful Bible verses

But you are God's chosen and special people. You are a group of royal priests and a holy nation. God has brought you out of darkness into his marvellous light.

1 PETER 2:9

He came into his own world, but his own nation did not welcome him. Yet some people accepted him and put their faith in him. So he gave them the right to be the children of God. They were not God's children by nature or because of any human desires. God himself was the one who made them his children.

JOHN 1:11–13

Can anything separate us from the love of Christ?

ROMANS 8:35

To consider

- As God's children, we belong to him and to one another as members of his body. We are all on his family tree.
- We can belong to earthly families, to spiritual families and to a global family.

- It is important to recognise that belonging brings with it a sense of responsibility. Just as God cares and provides for those who belong to him, so we should care for one another.
- We need to know who it is that we belong to. We can never fully know God this side of heaven, but it is important to find out and experience as much as we can. One of the ways we can find out about God is to study his names. We can only touch on a few of them in the session but your appetite might be whetted for further exploration.
- As God's children, we have a divine inheritance.

To discuss

- What helps people to feel that they belong?
- How can you establish a family identity and inclusive traditions?
- How can you welcome someone into your church family and make them feel integrated and valued?
- What do you think are the benefits of belonging to God?
- Is our divine inheritance for now or for eternity?

Session Two

Theme: Appropriate boundaries and encouragement

Helpful Bible verses

'Love the Lord your God with all your heart, soul, and mind… Love others as much as you love yourself.'
MATTHEW 22:37, 39

Teach your children right from wrong, and when they are grown they will still do right.
PROVERBS 22:6

Say the right thing at the right time and help others by what you say.
EPHESIANS 4:29

To consider

- Disciplining is a service that parents or people in authority can provide for those under their care, to encourage them to make good choices and develop a healthy conscience.
- God's discipline is consistent, fair and accompanied by a great deal of encouragement and affirmation.
- When we discipline, we need to be sure that there is a loving motivation and that a huge hug, a word of praise and a forgiving heart are always ready and waiting on the sidelines.
- God's rules are not intended to restrict us unnecessarily but to bring clarity and a sense of order.
- Appropriate boundaries and encouragement are like two sides of one coin, working together to produce a well-balanced person or a well-ordered community.
- The Ten Commandments are not obsolete. As Jesus came to fulfil the law and not to abolish it, we can assume that these commandments still have relevance for us today.

To discuss

- How do you consider the Ten Commandments still to have relevance today?
- How do you perceive discipline—as a negative thing or a positive one?
- Who should decide the boundaries in the various expressions of 'family'?
- What would your essential commandments be?
- How important is it to balance boundaries and encouragement?

Session Three

Theme: Valuing ourselves and others

Helpful Bible verses

Do your own work well, and then you will have something to be proud of. But don't compare yourself with others. We each must carry our own load.

GALATIANS 6:4–5

'You did not choose me. I chose you and sent you out to produce fruit, the kind of fruit that will last. Then my Father will give you whatever you ask for in my name. So I command you to love each other.'

JOHN 15:16–17

God has also given each of us different gifts to use. If we can prophesy, we should do it according to the amount of faith we have. If we can serve others, we should serve. If we can teach, we should teach. If we can encourage others, we should encourage them. If we can give, we should be generous. If we are leaders, we should do our best. If we are good to others, we should do it cheerfully.

ROMANS 12:6–8

To consider

- Bearing fruit is a natural progression in the life of trees. They cannot make themselves bear fruit or, indeed, choose the fruit that they will bear.
- Given the right conditions, they will automatically produce fruit according to their kind.
- God has instilled within each of us 'fruit' of some sort—a gifting or ability that is to be used to benefit others.
- Because they 'fit' us, we should enjoy our gifts.
- True happiness lies in being content with what we have. When we compare ourselves with others, it rarely has a helpful outcome.
- We should ensure that all gifts are equally valued and work to avoid a hierarchy in the way we view our gifts, not confusing function and status.

To discuss

- How can we encourage one another to discover and develop our gifts?
- Do we unintentionally place a higher value on some gifts than others?
- How can we learn to work together with those whose opinions, tastes and personalities may clash with our own?
- Do we leave space within our families and churches for members to explore their potential?

Session Four

Theme: Sharing what we have

Helpful Bible verses

Jesus looked up and saw some rich people tossing their gifts into the offering box. He also saw a poor widow putting in two pennies. And he said, 'I tell you that this poor woman has put in more than all the others. Everyone else gave what they didn't need. But she is very poor and gave everything she had.'

LUKE 21:1–4

'You received without paying, now give without being paid.'

MATTHEW 10:8B

'If your Lord and teacher has washed your feet, you should do the same for each other. I have set the example, and you should do for each other exactly what I have done for you.'

JOHN 13:14–15

To consider

- Sharing can include a smile, a word of encouragement, finance, resources, time, mentoring or role-modelling.
- There is nothing so small or seemingly insignificant that God can't use it. God is not limited by the amount we have to offer, only by the attitude in which the offering is made.
- Large oak trees begin life as little acorns.
- Consider God's abundance in the story of the feeding of the five thousand. He is undoubtedly a master mathematician and could have calculated how much food would be needed to the nearest crumb, yet we see twelve basketsful left over. What a wonderful picture of his abundant, overflowing giving!
- We need good role models and spiritual parents.
- Our giving can have a ripple effect, sometimes achieving far more than we could have anticipated.

To discuss

- How infectious is a smile? Try it out and see!
- Do you take time to receive in order to be able to give?
- What opportunities are there in our church families for mentoring?
- What does it take to be a spiritual parent or a good role model?
- Do we make room for our 'little acorns' to offer what they have?

Session Five

Theme: Resting on God's promises

Helpful Bible verses

I will bless those who trust me. They will be like trees growing beside a stream—trees with roots that reach down to the water, and with leaves that are always green. They will bear fruit every year and are never worried by a lack of rain.

JEREMIAH 17:7–8

The Lord is a mighty tower where his people can run for safety...

PROVERBS 18:10

The Lord is always kind to those who worship him, and he keeps his promises to their descendants.

PSALM 103:17

To consider

- We can know freedom from worry and fear, despite circumstances, because God has promised to be always 'watching our back'.
- Even when we fall, underneath us are the everlasting arms.
- There are promises that we can claim for our families, in the assurance that God will honour them.
- When Jesus taught the disciples how to address God, he used an expression that is the equivalent of our contemporary word 'Daddy'.
- We have plenty to celebrate.

To discuss

- How difficult is it to trust God for our families?
- Do you think God means it when he tells us not to worry?
- What promises has God given you?
- What do you think 'blessing' means?
- Do you take time as a family (or a church) to have fun and relax together?

Team building and preparation

Where do we begin when we want to gather together an enthusiastic, committed and gifted team, a fit-for-purpose body of people who will ensure the smooth running of our event? As each team will be unique (and hurrah for that!) there is no set formula. However, you may find it helps if you:

- share your vision enthusiastically, honestly and with a degree of clarity. Enthusiasm and energy are very contagious but some people like clear information as well.
- make sure people know that if they simply express an interest, they are not going to be pressganged into an immediate commitment.
- keep an eye out for people who might be too shy or self-effacing to put themselves forward and (without using the afore-mentioned coercion) encourage them to get involved if they're available.
- produce a rough timetable estimating the number of pre-event meetings that will be held, giving prospective dates where possible.
- remain open to suggestions.

In true matchmaking style, your team will need to fit the following profile: gsoh, lG, pf, av & w (great sense of humour, love God, people-friendly, available & willing). The good news is that, in keeping with one of the main themes of the programme, everyone has something to offer. The main roles needing to be fulfilled are as follows, although the make-up of your team may differ according to how you decide to organise your event, and some of the roles may overlap.

- Decision-making core group, who will take responsibility for the overall organisation and running of the event
- Up-front team, who are willing to introduce and lead activities
- Group and craft leaders who can facilitate discussion sensitively
- Refreshments team
- Registration team

- First aiders
- Storytellers
- Setter-uppers
- Drama team
- Puppeteers

The number of people you require for each role will depend upon how long your event will run for and the availability of people to fill the various slots.

Chinese shouts

At the outset, it is worth setting out clear lines of communication. In this situation, too much is better than too little, as it is preferable to tell a couple of people the same thing twice than to leave someone out of the loop. While the latter creates a fantastic opportunity for the 'overlooked' not to take offence and to practise a gracious attitude, it can be upsetting, time-consuming and problematic.

You could set up a 'news tree' so that the load is shared and everyone is covered. (Someone sends out a message from the root to a few branches, who then pass it on to some more branches, and so on until everyone has been notified. It's rather like a prayer chain, but that doesn't sound so agricultural!) Make sure everyone knows well ahead of time what they will be responsible for, and that they have everything they need to do the job properly.

Pray together as often as you can—and, finally, have fun! Remember that a picture paints a thousand words and our attitude could well be a 'picture' to someone.

Preparing the ground

When you have got your core team in place, you will need to make some key decisions, such as the 'shape' of your event, dates, venue, time of day and whether or not you will require people to pre-register. You need to ponder the reason why you are holding the event, who you want to reach, how wide you will cast your publicity net and what your budget is. What provisions will you make for refreshments? Consider also whether you will want to be proactive in publicising the event in previously 'un-networked' areas.

Check what facilities there are for waste disposal, as you may have a fair amount of rubbish to process—remembering to recycle wherever possible. Speaking of recycling, collect lots of junk. Make sure you give people plenty of notice to start setting aside any particular items you would like them to save.

Ask if anyone has any family-friendly DVDs, board games, jigsaws and so on that they would be willing to loan to you. Make sure these items are named and that there is nothing too precious in the collection. Encourage people only to lend what they wouldn't find too disastrous to lose. Obviously, you will take as good care of people's possessions as you can, but, with the best will in the world, accidents do sometimes happen.

Bibles would also be a very useful addition to your 'take away' section, as some families may not have access to one at home.

Health and safety

Think about how many people your venue can safely accommodate. Also, check with your church council, denominational body or local authority how many people will need to apply for a Criminal Records Bureau (CRB) check, and budget accordingly. Remember that organisers of meetings are responsible for ensuring that fire and other conditions attached to the use of the meeting place are not infringed. If the venue you are using is not familiar to you, make sure you check the regulations. Be sure to take into account any special needs you may have to accommodate.

Registration

Registration is a very necessary part of any event in order to ascertain whether everyone has got out safely in the event of a fire or other emergency. It can't be done frivolously but you could make the transition from registration to activity zone more exciting by perhaps including various-sized footprints, cut from coloured paper, leading from one to the other, emphasising that all ages (and sizes of feet!) are welcome. If you are able to, it would be great to have the registration area included in any themed décor—in this case, trees, leaves, fruit and seeds.

As you will probably want to divide everyone into groups at some stage, it might be useful during registration to give out different coloured stickers, ensuring a relatively even split in numbers and, if at all feasible, ages. Families should be kept together as far as possible. It might be worth displaying a timetable or two around the reception area so that everyone knows roughly what to expect.

'Welcome' activities

Set up enough seating facing your 'stage' area to accommodate both adults and children. In order to allow for the time taken to register people, and for those who may be a little late, set up some stalls around the peripheral area. Wherever possible, use adult-sized tables and chairs. The activities on the stalls can occupy the early birds while they await the arrival of the not-so-earlies. The stalls could offer simple, traditional family entertainment such as pin the tail on the donkey (or a themed version of the game), guess the number of seeds in a packet, guess the name of the teddy bear and so on. There may be a local school that has table games tucked away for use at school fêtes. If you ask nicely, they may let you borrow them.

There are suggestions in the 'Craft activities' section for a quick craft for each session, and this could be an opportune time to set it up. Also, it would be fun to have a joke book corner, filled with family-friendly books that can be scoured for jokes to be shared later in the session. You could display the verse 'If you are cheerful, you feel good' (Proverbs 17:22) and provide a receptacle into which suitable jokes could be posted.

In the seating area, have copies of the relevant wordsearch and colouring sheet available (see pages 125–129 and 134–138), along with some colouring pens and pencils. People might be encouraged to complete these sheets if they form part of a challenge, with a small reward for all correctly completed entries.

Make sure you provide a set place where people can leave any finished (or unfinished) articles that they would like to take home, and provide bags to put them in, if necessary. Decide on a signal to be given when you are about to start your programme. If you have advertised a time to start, try to stick to it, to prevent anyone from getting in a tizzy.

There will also be a few further practical considerations: for those, I'll hand you over to Ted. Ted is one of the characters who features in the puppet sketches, a salt-of-the-earth allotment holder who has for many years been the chairman of the AHS (the Allotment Holders' Society), and he has agreed to share the fruits of his vast experience with us.

Ted's top tips

1. Hold a health and safety check or risk assessment inspection.

Ted says: I know 'elf and safety' gets up everybody's nose a bit these days. It can be a reet nuisance, but it will prevent such embarrassing incidents as the one we had back in 1987 when young Pauline Scott tripped over a curled-up carpet edge, tipped the jug of water she were carrying on Sid's head and landed up on Gary Sugden's knee. She were the colour of beetroot. However, it did have a happy ending as she and Gary were married the next July.

2. Make sure everybody knows the whereabouts of the fire extinguishers and fire exits and that they know the drill in the event of a fire.

Ted says: We were very fortunate to have Miss Catherine Everard as part of our society for many years, as she had been a hair stewardess and, when she went through the fire drill with us, she were ever so elegant, even taking into account the blue rinse and the Nora Batty stockings. Lent a right air of sophistication to our proceedings, she did.

3. Give out name labels.

Ted says: This is essential to prevent a repeat of a particularly unpleasant occurrence at one of our AGMs. No one had thought to label committee members and so old Mrs Barrett, who was very hard of hearing, says in a voice that could shatter rock, 'Who's that lad up there with ears like the FA cup and a nose you could use ter open bottles?' She was of course referring to young Terry, and to be fair it was a very apt description, but the lad were so mortified, he gave up his allotment very shortly after and joined the Foreign Legion.

4. Provide toilet facilities.

Ted says: If you've folk at either end of the age spectrum coming to your meeting, you'll want to be sure there's enough WCs to accommodate them. With a lot of our older members, the tea seems to go in one end and out the other with unseemly haste. And, of course, nappies shouldn't be left unchanged. Not even George's famous Eastern Spices pot pourri is much use then.

5. Signpost parking facilities (for cars and pushchairs).

Ted says: Better let people know what the parking is like where you're going to be holding your event, just in case you've got a jobsworth like Gerald Moffett, our resident traffic warden, around. He has been known to hide behind bushes waiting to catch people out. In fact, the last time he did that, he trod on Madge Winter's cat, which let out an almighty yelp and so Madge chased him down t' road with a sweeping brush! He's retired now but we let him help park the pushchairs ('cos we get quite a lot of these organic-thinking young families at our meetings now), so he's happy. We even let him give out a parking ticket now and again if they park in front of fire exits. Then he's very happy.

6. Don't forget to leave space for crafts to dry.

Ted says: You don't want those lovely creations getting ruined or it'll end in tears. Which reminds me, don't forget to 'ave some hankies around. There's nothing worse than seeing a 'slimy slug trail' on a youngster's sleeve. Or a granny's.

7. Put up a timetable.

Ted says: That'll be your fancy name for the agenda, as I'd call it. That way, everyone knows where they are, or where they should be if they're not. If you know what I mean.

Starter activities

First of all, to set the scene, it would be good to have the décor of your venue reflecting the overall theme of trees, to a greater or a lesser extent. There are large inflatable trees available for hire or purchase, or you could design your very own custom-made trees, using, for example, the large cardboard tubes that can be obtained from carpet shops, or the skeletons of old umbrellas, decorated with colourful pieces of fabric, leaf shapes and so on. You could have strings of leaves hanging from the ceiling, creating a sense of being in a shady bower. Alternatively, you might just want to have a couple of visually striking wall-mounted displays, using simple shapes and coloured paper.

You will need to have one tree available to show the various life stages in action. Again, this could be a two-dimensional display, with additions made to it session by session (for example, young tree; sacking round the base; fruit; seeds; person resting against it), or you might like to set aside a small area, put down some fake grass or green fabric and create a three-dimensional display. Or, indeed, let your artistic members use their imagination and lots of junk!

Below are some starter activities for introducing the session themes. You might like to use them to expand on the idea glanced at in the puppet sketches, or in place of the puppet sketches as a starting point for your programme. It would be useful to have your 'tree visual' somewhere close to hand.

Session One: The tree is planted

Bible link

Can anything separate us from the love of Christ?

ROMANS 8:35

In this session, we're thinking about what it means to belong. Just as our tree has been planted in good soil, God has planted us, and the Bible tells us that we belong to him. One of the most fantastic things about belonging to God is that nothing can separate us from him.

Show a container with undiluted squash in it and a jug of water. You might like to get some volunteers from the audience to help you, to check that the squash is real and so forth. Mix the squash and the water together and ask if anyone has any ideas about how they could be separated out again. It is not possible. Isn't that wonderful?

Session Two: The sapling tree

Bible link

Teach your children right from wrong, and when they are grown they will still do right.

PROVERBS 22:6

In this session, we're going to be thinking about the importance of having some rules and also the importance of encouragement. Our tree has something around its base, which is there to help protect it from anything that might harm it while it's growing. In the same way, rules can help us stay safe. God's rules are always good rules, intended to help us live in harmony with him and with one another. However, sometimes people make rules that are a bit silly.

Ask for volunteers to make up a couple of teams. Divide your audience into two parts, each part supporting one of the teams. Read out the list of rules (laws) on page 122 and invite the teams to take turns in guessing which is the real law. They can ask their own part of the audience to help them.

Session Three: The tree bears fruit

Bible link

Do your own work well, and then you will have something to be proud of. But don't compare yourself with others. We each must carry our own load.

GALATIANS 6:4–5

The theme here is about enjoying who we are and not comparing ourselves with other people. Just as our tree has some fruit on it, God gives each of us the ability to bear fruit—that is, to be able to do something for him—and he wants us to be content with what he's given us, because he loves us all equally.

Ask for volunteers to come and act out the following charades and see if the audience can guess what the charade is.

- Passionate preaching
- Making a cup of tea
- Working in an office
- Acting a tragic scene in a play
- Building a wall
- Sewing the hem on a dress

Mention that all these activities can be important. It's not what we do that matters; it's how we do it.

Session Four: The tree sends out seeds

Bible link

You received without paying, now give without being paid.

MATTHEW 10:8B

In this session, our tree has sent out some seeds. So now, more trees will grow. Did you know that we all have seeds we can send out? It might be some money we can send to people who don't have as much as we do, or it might be something much simpler, like a kind word.

Show four seed-shaped cards, each with one of the following actions written on it, and explain that you are going to be sending some seeds out to see if they spread.

- A big smile
- A handshake
- A friendly wave
- Blow a kiss

Give one of the cards to someone at each of the four corners (or equivalent) of your audience. Ask those people to pass on the action that is written on their card (they don't need to pass on the card itself), and see if you can get the whole audience smiling, waving and so on. You may need to suggest a direction to each of the corners—for example, 'pass it on to the person on your left (or right)'. It might get a bit messy in the middle, but that doesn't matter. It should be a happy mess!

Session Five: The tree in maturity

Bible link

I will bless those who trust me. They will be like trees growing beside a stream—trees with roots that reach down to the water, and with leaves that are always green. They will bear fruit every year and are never worried by a lack of rain.

JEREMIAH 17:7–8

Look at our fully grown tree! Now we can relax: we could lie down under it and enjoy the shade, or we could play on it because it looks very sturdy and safe. God loves us to relax and play. He wants us to know that he is in control so we don't have to worry, because we can trust him completely. The Bible tells us that even if things go wrong, God will be there with us. That's something to celebrate, so let's get some party food out and find some volunteers to eat it.

Have a table or two set up with some suitably messy food, a spoon and an old shirt to serve as an apron. One of your volunteers will be the arms and the other will be the mouth. Working together, they will attempt to eat the food. You might like to do this as a race between two pairs. A plastic cloth under the table(s) might be a good idea.

Obviously, when God is in charge, he doesn't make a mess of things, but he does love us to have fun!

Craft activities

For each session, there are suggested crafts together with ideas for discussion starters. The crafts are not too simple, in the hope that that might encourage parents and children to work together. Set them out on adult-sized tables, as even young children adapt well to this, while adults do not take kindly to sitting on tiny chairs. You will need to have at least one helper at each table in case you have non-readers or people who might struggle with the language or with interpreting a large amount of text.

You might want to make a sign that indicates if the craft will need adult help (for example, a big person and little person), some laminated instructions and a relevant Bible verse to help direct the chat (see below). Remember to leave space and time for finished items to dry, and ensure that everything is named.

The longer crafts should take about 15 to 20 minutes each. However, as the time taken over crafts can be variable and you don't want to hold up the programme too much, it might be an idea to have bags and printed instructions available, so that people can take home the constituent parts if they don't complete the craft there and then.

With each craft, there should be some suggestions for discussion starters, produced on laminated sheets if possible, to enable anyone in the group to initiate discussion. Also there should be a printed set of instructions so that adults are not reliant on a helper to begin the craft.

Session One: The tree is planted

Quick craft

Draw the outline of a tree trunk on a large piece of paper or card. Underneath, write 'God's family tree'. Provide green paint, some thick paintbrushes, a bowl of soapy water and some paper towels. Invite each person to paint their hand green and add their handprint to God's family tree, their handprints forming the leaves.

Bible link

Yet some people accepted him and put their faith in him. So he gave them the right to be the children of God.

JOHN 1:12

The bunting of belonging

You will need:

Triangles cut from A4 sheets of coloured paper, with about 2cm turned over at the top edge to allow for the string to pass through; photocopied sheets with various useful symbols such as a person shape, a jumper, a flag, a badge, common domestic animals, a place of worship, sports equipment; paper for people to create their own symbols; scissors (child- and adult-sized); coloured pencils; PVA glue; glue spreaders; string to join them all together; a stapler; a completed piece of bunting as an example; a laminated sheet with the Bible link verse

---

Bible link

You are God's chosen and special people.

1 PETER 2:9

Explain what bunting is or have some hanging up nearby. Invite everyone to make their very own piece of bunting. It should show some of the things they belong to as a family and some of the things that belong to each person as individuals. Chat about what's good about belonging to something and how we should treat the things that belong to us.

Laminated instructions

Choose symbols of things that apply to you as a family or make some of your own. Stick them on to the piece of bunting.

When everyone has completed their piece of bunting, staple the turned-down edges, join the triangles together with the string and display where everyone can see the finished result.

Name jewellery

You will need:

Something on to which to thread your 'beads', such as thin elastic; wool; fishing line or dental floss; paperclips to use as a 'bead stopper'; a selection of beads, including alphabet ones or dried pasta, such as macaroni which has a smooth surface to write on; dark coloured felt-tipped pens for writing on pasta; a sheet with some of the names of God on it (see page 124); a finished example of a bracelet; laminated instructions sheet

The idea is to make a bracelet that includes either people's first name or their initials as part of the pattern. This can be done in a variety of ways, some cheaper than others. If you have a small group, you might like to buy supplies from a craft shop. However, if your group is larger and money is limited, you have the advantage of being able to use your imagination and make your jewellery even more personal.

NB: The pasta can be coloured in advance to make it more attractive. This is done by soaking it in rubbing alcohol (surgical spirit) coloured with food colouring (just enough in a bowl to cover the pasta) for about 15 minutes (covered). Drain off the alcohol mixture and put the pasta on to paper towels to dry. Using wax paper may prevent the pasta from sticking to the paper but can allow the colour to run. Alternatively, the pasta can be coloured with felt-tipped pens or paint.

Laminated instructions

Make a bracelet that includes your name or initials. Cut a piece of elastic or wool long enough to go round your wrist, with enough left over to fasten it. Place a paperclip at one end to act as a 'bead stop'. Select the beads or pasta that you want to use, making sure you write your name or initials on one or two pieces of pasta. When you have completed your pattern, if you are using elastic, tie the ends together in a knot and cut off any excess. However, if you are using wool, you will need to get someone to help you tie it in a bow.

To chat about

Do you know what your name means? If you could choose your own name, what would it be? Think about how many names God has. Which one is your favourite? Why?

Session Two: The sapling tree

Quick craft

Provide some clay or playdough and some cocktail sticks. Give everyone a small piece to make into a brick shape, on to which they can 'write' their name or initials or a symbol. (Be careful of sharp points with little people.) All the bricks can then be put together to build a wall.

Talk about how walls are sometimes needed to keep harmful things away from crops or animals. Talk about how God's rules are like walls, helping to keep us safe. Do we need rules in our families that help to keep us safe?

Commandment hangings

You will need:
Heart shapes, approximately 10cm high, cut out of pink or red card; person shapes of various colours, approximately 15cm tall; pink and red tissue paper cut into small squares; various skin tones of tissue paper cut into small squares; hole punch; approximately 15cm lengths of thin ribbon; PVA glue; glue spreaders; scissors (adult); a finished example of each ornament; laminated instructions sheet; laminated Bible link verse

Bible link
Love the Lord your God with all your heart, soul, and mind... Love others as much as you love yourself.
MATTHEW 22:37, 39

Laminated instructions

Make two lovely ornaments to hang in your home to remind you of the two helpful rules that Jesus said were the most important ones. With the hole punch, make a hole at the top centre of the cut-out shape. Roll pieces of the coloured tissue paper into little balls, then spread some glue on to part of the shape and glue the tissue paper on, until the whole shape is covered. An adult may like to trim around the shape to make sure it looks neat. Thread some ribbon through the hole at the top and tie into a bow. You might like to write the appropriate Bible verse on the back.

To chat about

How can we show God that we love him with every part of us? What sort of things could we do to show love to the people around us? Who is our neighbour? Could it be a member of our family?

Pompoms of encouragement

You will need:
Oblongs of plastic approximately 30cm x 10cm in assorted colours, cut from bin bags, carrier bags or thin plastic tablecloths (you will need about 20 per person and the strips in the instructions below could be pre-cut for children); electrical tape or similar; scissors (adult); laminated instruction sheet; laminated Bible link verse

Bible link

Say the right thing at the right time and help others by what you say.
EPHESIANS 4:29

NB: You could use ready-shredded coloured paper instead of plastic, but it doesn't shake quite so well.

Until the 1920s, cheerleading was largely a male and all-American activity.

A useful standby chant is: '2, 4, 6, 8, who do I appreciate?'

Laminated instructions

Make a pompom and invent your own cheerleader chant to encourage someone. Lay the oblongs on top of each other, alternating the colours, and cut into five strips, 30cm x 2cm. Gather them together by grasping them into a fist at the centre. Use electrical tape or similar to wrap tightly around the strips, making a 'handle' in the centre of approximately 5cm. Separate the strips by peeling them towards the centre and fluff them out until you have a pompom. Use your pompom to tell someone how much you appreciate them.

To chat about

How do you feel when someone says something encouraging to you? Think about the way you speak to your family and friends. Could you encourage them more?

Session Three: The tree bears fruit

Quick craft

Make a plant pot out of newspaper by folding a piece of newspaper into a long strip, about 15cm wide. Take a glass jar and lay it on its side at one end of the strip of paper, with about half the width of the newspaper overlapping the open end of the jar. Roll the newspaper around the jar and then stuff the overlapping paper into the open end of the jar. Remove the jar and place it into your 'paper pot', pressing it down in order to flatten the bottom of the pot. Remove the jar and, hey presto, a biodegradable pot! Now you can put some potting soil in it. Plant a bulb in the pot.

To chat about

Chat about all the good things that God has planted in each one of us. Although a bulb doesn't look much like the flower it will grow into, we just need to look at the packet and have faith that the beautiful flower is in there, waiting to come out. Isn't it wonderful that, when God looks at us, he sees all our potential, not our limitations?

Windmills

You will need:
Coloured paper (not too flimsy), cut into squares 14cm x 14cm; garden sticks; corks; tape; dressmaking pins with beaded heads; small beads, buttons or 1cm pieces cut from a drinking straw; decorations; a completed windmill; laminated instruction sheet

Laminated instructions

Fold your paper, corner to opposite corner, making a triangular shape. Press down the crease, then unfold. Repeat with the other two corners. From each corner, cut towards the centre to a distance of about 7cm (just over halfway to the centre). Put a small mark in each corner, to the right of the cut. Lay the paper to one side for a moment or decorate if desired.

Take a cork and tape it to one end of a stick. Take your paper, fold the edges that you marked into the centre and hold them there with a dressmaking pin. Slide a small bead or button on to the pin, or put the pin through the piece of straw and then press the pin into the cork. You should now have a windmill.

To chat about

Trees need to breathe air in order to stay alive. Wind is air moving from one place to another. When you have made your windmill, blow on it to make it spin. Can you see the air that is making it move? Can you think of any other important things that are invisible?

Seed mosaic

You will need:
One simple outline drawing on card for every 6–8 people; a selection of as many different sorts and colours of seeds, rice and pulses as you can find (rice, beans, birdseed, corn kernels and sunflower seeds are examples of seeds that you can use); PVA glue; glue spreaders or brushes; small spoons; varnish (optional); laminated instruction sheet; laminated Bible link verse

Bible link

Do your own work well, and then you will have something to be proud of. But don't compare yourself with others. We each must carry our own load.

GALATIANS 6:4–5

Laminated instructions

Working as a team, choose the best seeds for each part of the picture and glue them carefully on to the card. When completed, you could finish with a coat of varnish. Enjoy the work of art you have created by working together.

To chat about

Look at the amazing variety of colours, shapes and sizes! Do you like finding out about people who are different from you? In what ways are the people in your family different? In what ways are they alike?

Session Four: The tree sends out seeds

Quick craft

Provide biscuits or small cakes, coloured icing and sweets or decorations. Also provide some kitchen roll or small paper plates. Invite everyone to decorate their cake or biscuit as beautifully as they can and then give it to someone else to bless them.

To chat about

Talk about how lovely it feels when someone gives you an unexpected gift.

Family photo tree

You will need:
A variety of tree trunk shapes cut from brown paper (make sure they each have five roots, spread out enough to allow symbols to be stuck on them); a variety of leaf shapes cut from leaf-coloured paper; coloured card; printed sheet with the following symbols on it, drawn small enough to fit at the end of the tree roots after they have been cut out: a hand, a speech bubble, a thought bubble, a heart, a sharing sign (mathematical division sign with smiley faces instead of dots); PVA glue; glue spreaders; aluminium foil (optional); laminated instruction sheet; laminated Bible link verse

Bible link
You received without paying, now give without being paid.

MATTHEW 10:8B

Laminated instructions

Choose a trunk and lots of leaf shapes to make your unique 'family tree'. Glue them on to the card, leaving enough space at the bottom to glue on the symbols. The symbols should remind us to do, say and think things that will bless our family, as follows:

- Hand: what we do
- Speech bubble: what we say
- Thought bubble: how we think
- Heart: how we feel
- Sharing sign: being willing to share what we have

Take some extra leaf shapes home with you and find photos of your family that are small enough to fit on the leaves (you may need to cut them, but be sure to check with the owner of the photo first). Roll some silver foil into a very thin 'worm' and glue around the individual photos to frame them. Add them to your tree.

To chat about

Families, like trees, come in all shapes and sizes. Is your family like a young tree or can you trace it a long way back in time? Name all the 'families' you are part of (school, church, global and so on). What do you think the symbols could mean?

Rockin' person award

You will need:
The figure template on page 131 photocopied on to card; coloured paper or a selection of fabric scraps; colouring pens; PVA glue; glue spreaders; laminated instruction sheet

Laminated instructions

Decorate the figure on the card using the pens, fabric and so on. Cut out the two sides and stick the top halves together. The bottom halves should be spread out so that the figure stands up and rocks. Give your rockin' person award to someone you think really rocks!

To chat about

Think about all the people who have taught you something. Is there anyone who has helped you by being really kind? Have you ever been given a certificate or award? What do you think a blessing is?

Session Five: The tree in maturity

Quick craft

With gold pen or felt-tipped pens, ask everyone to write their name on a balloon and choose some coloured curling ribbon to make a tail. Blow up the balloons (if you want to push the boat out, you could use helium gas), and keep them in black sacks.

To chat about

Talk about how we can sometimes feel 'flat' or deflated, but, when we think about all the promises God has made, it lifts us up.

Later, if you're going to be eating, use the balloons as place markers, ensuring that there is a good mix of people at each table. If you are not eating together, give the balloons out as people leave.

Balloon party plate mosaic

You will need:
Paper plates with the outline of a balloon drawn on each one; lots of magazines and brightly coloured paper; thin ribbon; scissors; PVA glue; glue spreaders; equal parts PVA glue and water mixture to use as a seal (optional); brushes; laminated instruction sheet; laminated Bible link verse

Bible link
The Lord is faithful to all his promises and loving toward all he has made.
PSALM 145:13B (NIV 1984)

Laminated instructions

Cut out lots of small squares from the coloured paper. Carefully glue your squares to the plate, inside the balloon shape. Add a ribbon 'tail' to your balloon. When your pattern or picture is complete, you might like to seal it with a glue-and-water mixture. When it is completely dry, put some party food on it and have a celebration.

To chat about
Isn't it great to celebrate that we have a faithful God? Did you know that the rainbow was a sign that God would never break his promise to Noah? Think about the things that worry you. Why not ask someone if there is a promise God has made that might help you to stop worrying?

Promise boxes

You will need:
Copies of the net on page 132 printed out on to thin card or thick paper, or a selection of small used boxes that can be covered; wrapping paper to cover used boxes; scissors (adult); glue sticks or PVA glue; felt-tipped pens; decorations such as stickers and ribbons; laminated instruction sheet; laminated Bible link verse

Bible link
The Lord is faithful to all his promises and loving toward all he has made.
PSALM 145:13B (NIV 1984)

Laminated instructions

If using the net, cut out and stick together as indicated, being careful not to stick down the lid. Decorate as desired. If using the used boxes, cover with patterned paper and add stickers and ribbons to make them really special.

To chat about
Talk about verses in the Bible that contain promises God has made. Write some of God's promises on to slips of paper to keep in your promise box. Write out promises that you can give to family members on special occasions. An example might be 'I promise to clean the bathroom this week' or 'I promise to read you a story every night this week.' Keep them in your promise box and bring out when appropriate.

Team challenges

Each team challenge lasts between 15 and 20 minutes. For the challenges (or games), you will need to divide people into groups. If they were given stickers at registration, this will make the task easier. Another way of attempting to get a mix of ages in your groups would be to line people up in height order and then number them off from one to however many groups you want. You then gather all the number ones together and so on. It's not perfect, but it will at least jumble people up a bit. If you have time at the end, spend a couple of minutes talking about the 'chatlines' suggested at the end of each activity.

Session One: The tree is planted
Think about... what it means to belong.

Matching pairs

Give each team a digital camera and allow ten minutes for them to photograph as many pairs that belong together as possible—for example, a shoe and a sock; a pen and a piece of paper. Define the area(s) where they are allowed to look. They must return as soon as you signal the end of the ten-minute period.

Look at each other's findings. The winning team is the one with the most pairs. Allow unusual pairs as long as the team has a good or amusing explanation for why they belong together.

Alternatively, have lots of photos of things that belong together hidden around the venue and give the teams ten minutes to see who can find the most. If you are doing this one team at a time, note how many photos each team finds and work out the winning team at the end.

Chatline
How do we decide what things belong together?

Belonga conga

Ask everyone to get into a circle and think about their name. Go around the circle and ask each person to say their name and something they belong to or really enjoy, accompanying their words with a simple action. If you have more than 20 people in your group, divide into more than one circle.

Everyone in the circle then moves clockwise, maintaining the circle, in a conga rhythm, repeating the name and activity—for example, 'Rajan does karate; Kevin's in a golf club; Emma goes to Slimming World'—keeping the rhythm as best they can. When everyone has done this, choose someone to be the leader and break into a traditional conga line. Conga round the room with people calling out their name and activity in turn, starting with the leader and moving in order down the line, keeping the conga rhythm going at all times.

Chatline
Why do people join clubs or groups?

Session Two: The sapling tree

Think about... how helpful it is to be given clear instructions.

Set up a couple of identical obstacle courses, using cones or chairs. Ask teams to direct one another, in pairs, around a pre-set course, with one person being blindfolded, the other using their voice. There could be two or three tasks that they have to complete en route, such as putting beanbags into a bucket, collecting an item, eating some marshmallows or drawing something simple. (Make sure someone is on hand to reset the course each time.) The winning team is the one that gets all its members through the course in the shortest time, having completed all the tasks.

Chatline
What was the most difficult thing about being a guide or being guided?

Marble run

> **You will need:**
> Lots of cardboard or plastic tubes and any other useful junk you can find;
> a number of marbles; sticky tape; scissors; colouring pens and pencils

Divide into teams of four to six people and see which team can make the most interesting (and working) marble run in ten minutes. If you have a lot of teams, shorten the time allowed for building, making sure there is time at the end to try out the runs. Emphasise that all team members should be included.

Chatline
What helped to keep the marbles travelling along the right path?

Session Three: The tree bears fruit

Think about... variety.

Moving fruit

At one end of the room, place a number of coloured balls or screwed-up balls of coloured paper to represent fruit. At the other end, place a circle (perhaps a hoop or a chalked circle) marked 'fruit bowl', large enough to contain all the balls.

The object is to move the fruit from one end to the other without using your hands. Fan with a newspaper or pizza box; dribble with your feet; push with your nose; carry between your knees, on a spoon, under your chin or on a tennis racquet; shuffle on your bottom; sweep with a broom; walk backwards. Tell your groups that they can add other suggestions, but that they can only use each method once (unless there are more team players than methods, in which case methods may be repeated).

Teams may need a few minutes to decide who will do what. If they drop the ball, they must come back to the beginning and start again or incur a ten-second penalty. The winning team is the one that moves all the fruit to the fruit bowl in the quickest time.

Chatline
Why do you think there are so many types of fruit?

Fruit salad plus

Make a circle of chairs with a clear space in the middle. Have one less chair than the number of participants in the group. If there are many more than 20 people in the group, make more than one circle. Go around the circle, giving everyone the name of one of four fruits: apple, banana, cherry or grape.

Whoever is leading the game should stand in the middle and call out one of the fruit names; then everyone who was given that name has to move to a different chair. At this point, the person in the middle can try to get on to a chair, and whoever is left standing becomes the new leader. If the leader calls out 'fruit salad', everyone has to move.

As you will be playing this game with a mixed age group, you might like to make the extra rule that there are speed controls 1–3. Speed 1 is slow motion, speed 2 is walking pace and speed 3 is power walking. If you use this option, the leader will need to call out a number before calling out the fruit.

When you have played for a short while, explain to the grapes that when you call their fruit out, they must move into the middle and get themselves into a big bunch, all joining hands as quickly as possible. They will be representing joyfulness, one of the fruits of the Holy Spirit, as they will all be joined happily together. The cherries must move to the middle and get into pairs with hands joined like two cherries joined together, as that is often how you find them. They represent faithfulness. (If there is an odd number, there can be three cherries in a group.) The apples and bananas move into the middle as individuals, each making a relevant shape. The apples represent goodness ('an apple a day keeps the doctor away'), and the bananas represent kindness, as they are quite soft!

When you have called out each fruit (and fruit salad) a few times, try calling out the quality rather than the fruit name. (During this second part of the game, they do not need to scramble for chairs, as the leader will remain the same throughout.)

Chatline

'The fruit of the Spirit is love, joy, peace, patience, kindness, goodness, faithfulness, gentleness and self-control.'
GALATIANS 5:22–23 (NIV 1984)

Which real fruits might represent the other fruits of the Spirit?

Session Four: The tree sends out seeds
Think about... doing our bit.

Balloon-blow football

Set out tables and chairs to accommodate the number of people in two teams. Tables should be arranged end to end, to form a long narrow row. Place an equal number of members from each team on either side of the table, sitting in alternate places (so that team members don't sit next to each other). Label one end of the table 'A' and the other end 'B'.

Explain that the aim is to score goals by blowing a balloon over the opposing team's goal line at the end of the table. Hands must be kept off the table and you must move the balloon only by blowing it. If you have a large group, you may want to set up more than one set of tables, or have more than one balloon in play at a time. Start by placing a balloon in the centre. Think about how one small puff of air probably won't move the balloon very far, but, with everyone adding their effort, it is possible to move it a long way.

Chatline
What was the most effective way of directing the balloon?

Making shapes

Get people moving around the room at different speeds; 1: freeze, 2: slow motion, 3: normal walking pace, 4: as fast as they can manage, being mindful of everyone else. Ask them to think about levels (high, low) and direction (left, right, up, down) as they move around the space. Get them to move by leading with different parts of their body—their nose, tummy or knees, perhaps—and to experiment with big movements and small movements.

When you have practised all this, tell them that, this time, as they are moving about, anyone can stop and make a shape with their body. When anyone becomes aware that someone has stopped, they should immediately add themselves to the shape until everyone is part of the 'sculpture'. Then, one by one, people start peeling off and resume moving around. When they've got the hang of this, put on some music and ask everyone to move around as before. Have a variety of excerpts of music, with different moods and rhythms.

Chatline
How did it feel to be part of a human sculpture?

Session Five: The tree in maturity
Think about... celebrating our faithful God.

The chocolate game

> **You will need:**
> For each group, several items of clothing, such as hat, gloves, scarf or crown, cloak; a dice; knife and fork; large bar of chocolate; wrapping paper

This game is a perennial party favourite, so it's a good one to use to emphasise that we are celebrating our faithful God. It picks up on the Bible verse 'Taste and see that the Lord is good' (Psalm 34:8, NIV 1984).

The bar of chocolate is wrapped with the wrapping paper several times over. The participants stand or sit in a circle around the wrapped chocolate bar. Each participant rolls the dice and the first to roll a six starts the game, putting on the items of clothing before attempting to eat the chocolate bar using the knife and fork.

The object of the game is to eat the whole chocolate bar. There is no real winner, but it can be played so that whoever takes the last bite of the chocolate bar wins.

As the dice continues around the circle, if another player rolls a six, they shout 'Six!' The player in the centre has to stop immediately and take off the game clothing to transfer to his or her successor, who puts on the clothing and attempts to eat the chocolate piece by piece until the next player rolls a six.

Chatline
What was the silliest part of the game?

Beat the goalie

Set up a goal and mark out a line behind which people must stand in order to shoot at the goal. If you are indoors, use a soft ball. You might like to have a line closer to the goal for the smaller participants. Each team should choose a goalie and the opposing team must try to get the ball past them. If there are several people who want a turn at being goalie, that's fine. Obviously, the winning team is the one with the most goals in the allotted time.

Chatline

It's great to celebrate when our team wins, but the Bible tells us that we can celebrate at any time, because 'if we confess our sins to God, he can always be trusted to forgive us and take our sins away' (1 John 1:9). When we do, say or think wrong things, it's a bit like having goals scored against us, but when we turn to Jesus, he's like the perfect goalie and he knocks the sin away. That way, with Jesus on our side, we're always on the winning team.

Stories

It's incredible to think that most of the stories in the Bible were originally passed down by word of mouth. It's equally amazing that we can continue that oral tradition by voicing our own stories, be they personal testimonies or new metaphors to help people understand the things of God.

Each generation will announce to the next your wonderful and powerful deeds. I will keep thinking about your marvellous glory and your mighty miracles.
PSALM 145:4–5

There is a tremendous power in narrative and metaphor, brought to life through nothing more than some vocal cords and several pairs of ears. I confess that my ears were keenly tuned in to a radio programme called *Listen with Mother* on a regular basis as a child, and I have adored listening to and reading stories ever since.

You may like to present the story to the whole group or to smaller groups, depending on how many people are attending your event. The intimacy in a smaller setting can be beneficial but, for some people, there is safety in numbers, so you will need to decide which is best for you and your group.

The stories take about ten minutes to present, depending on how long it takes to get everyone seated and listening. Their purpose is to highlight one aspect of the session theme in an engaging way and, as they are mostly interactive, they should ensure that your audience stays engaged. Suggestions for presentation are given; feel free, however, to do your own thing if you're more comfortable with that.

Storytelling tips

Do you feel anxious about the prospect of telling a story to a large group of people when you're not used to doing that sort of thing? Perhaps you don't really know how you managed to get volunteered to do it. You thought you were putting your hand up for coffee… Well, don't panic; help is at hand.

There is a marvellous exhortation in the Bible, repeated 366 times, so I'm told (once for every day of the year, even in leap years): 'Do not be afraid!' This is not a finger-wagging reprimand but an invitation to wallow in the freedom for which Jesus set us free, given by one who knows that he has us covered. Therefore, any reluctant storytellers among us can jump fearlessly into the deep end of our hesitation, in the certain knowledge that we will not be left to drown. We may only doggy-paddle our way to safety, but I have no doubt that God loves a cheerful doggy-paddler. And who knows, we may find ourselves walking on water.

For starters, we can all breathe. Breathing is a much underrated activity as an aid to relaxation—the sort of deep breathing that calms your nerves and gets oxygen flowing to the parts that might have been stagnating. Breathe in deeply for a count of ten and then slowly exhale. Repeat several times. This is a handy little technique and surprisingly effective. If we put that in our storyteller's toolkit, we'll be well on our way.

The second tool isn't quite so easy to handle, especially for those of us who lead ridiculously busy lives. Nevertheless, it is essential if we're serious about doing as good a job as we can—which isn't a bad idea, considering that we are encouraged to do everything in a way that is good and pleasing to God (Romans 12:2). The second tool is... practice. It is really important to go over and over something as often as we need to, in order to feel secure with it. There is no substitute; it is a discipline and one that yields results. Many performers will tell you that their minds go blank just before going on stage, and that can be a scary feeling. But if we are well rehearsed, a kind of auto-pilot takes over and the show does go on (hurrah!). When you are practising (as I hope you've now been persuaded to do), here are a few helpful tips:

- Read out loud to yourself.
- Practise in front of a mirror.
- Ask a friend to listen to you and give helpful advice.
- Practise with any props you will need on the day, so that any potential problems can be identified.
- Check the focal distance at which your script will be positioned (a music stand is a handy thing to have at this point), particularly if you're 'of a certain age'.

No one will expect you to learn the script, just to be really familiar with it. And you don't need be an actor of Shakespearean ability, just to read with expression.

Once you have rehearsed enough to have a rough idea of what might be coming next, you will be confident enough to take your eyes off the script to make eye contact with your audience. This does not need to be sustained contact with any individual, just a glancing around, lingering momentarily to the left, right and centre, so that everyone in the audience will feel included.

Now you'll really be on a roll, so you might like to consider a few vocal and facial warm-up exercises, as follows.

* Pretend you're eating very sticky toffee. Start with small chewing movements and build to really big ones, so that the whole of your jaw is getting a good workout.
* Take a deep breath and pant, using your diaphragm.
* Take some deep breaths and sigh them out.
* Encourage lip and tongue mobility by repeating a couple of tongue twisters a few times.

Tuck a little pace variation, occasional changes of pitch and maybe even the odd meaningful pause into your toolkit and you'll be 'good to go'. Most importantly, enjoy it. Audiences, like animals, can smell fear, so go back to the beginning of this section and enforce it immediately!

Anyway, in ten minutes or so, it'll all be over.

Session One: The tree is planted

God's names

You will need:

A globe; a pair of binoculars; an umbrella with some cardboard leaves dangling from the spokes; a small glass of water; a piece of bread; a baby doll; some filthy rags; a representation of a tree with 'Dad' written on the trunk and 'You and me' written on the leafy section

---

In advance, you will need to prepare a card for each of the featured names of God, along with the relevant meaning.

Gather your chosen props near you, with a table to one side on to which you can place them as indicated in the script. You may like to ask a helper from the audience to place the correct name card with the representative object. Alternatively, if you have the technical know-how, you might like to produce a PowerPoint presentation.

Mention that in this session we are thinking about what it means to belong, particularly to God's family tree. The Bible tells us that, as his children, we are called by his name. In the Bible, names are often used to describe something about the person they are given to: for example, Abraham means 'father of many nations'. Explain that you are going to tell a story based on some of God's names, so that we can discover more about the God to whom we belong.

In the nothingness, there was nothing. At. All. Nothing.

The silence was not a welcome rest from sound. It was nothing.

The dark was not a blanket cloaked around the light to lull us into sleep. It was nothing.

Then into the nothingness spoke the all-powerful one, the Creator, 'Elohim', who breathed into the nothing and formed…

Everything.

Pick up the globe and spin it, then put it down.

Green things, blue things, shiny, bright and new things.

Things with spots, things with stripes, things which crawl, things which fly.

Wet things, dry things, easy-on-the-eye things.

Hot things, cold things, young things, old things.

Trees that could have lived a thousand years, all in a moment—there! Just like that.

Ping!

Open the umbrella with fruit attached. Leave to one side.

So easily, 'Elohim' created… everything.

Place the globe on the table with the relevant card.

And everything he creates, even now, he loves and watches over…

Pick up the binoculars and look at the audience through them for a moment or two.

There! In the jostling schoolyard! And there, in that tick-tock, watch-the-clock office and over in the noisy factory! In the desert, in the brush, in the skyscraper-bordered rush, in every nook and cranny, watching every child and granny, the eyes of the God who sees, the eyes of 'El Roi'.

Full of compassion, feisty with love; searching, unblinking through space and time, eternally watching, always with an expression of deepest love.

Place the binoculars on to the table with card. Put your hand to your ear and listen.

Now, can you hear that? It's a murmur… a moaning, muttering murmur! Moan, moan, mutter, mutter, moan, moan, mutter, mutter… It's the people of Israel in the desert. They've come out of Egypt, come miraculously through the waters of the Red Sea like a knife through butter and… speaking of butter, now they're hungry, so it's moan, moan, mutter, mutter. They had food in Egypt but they've got none now. They're going to starve, aren't they? And what's more, they're thirsty, too. The water at Marah is bitter. They can't possibly drink that. Better off in Egypt! Moan, moan. Why should they stay here to die? Mutter, mutter. As this wispy, cloudy column of murmurs snakes its way to heaven, the God who provides for all our needs, 'Jehovah Jireh', is stirred into action.

He tells Moses how to make the bitter waters sweet with the branch of a tree, and sends down manna from heaven to feed the people.

Pick up the water and bread.

Every single day, food and water—just what they need. 'Jehovah Jireh' gives them each day their daily bread. And each day, if we come to him, he'll give us just what we need. Just for today. He can still make the bitter sweet in so many ways.

Place bread, water and card on the table. Use your arms to make a clock movement or move the hands on a clock, making sure you move in a clockwise direction from the audience's perspective.

Time passes and a new season begins. A name, a God-breathed word written in the scrolls of old, becomes flesh. A baby is born and God is with us: 'Emmanuel'!

Hold baby doll up in the air and gradually bring it lower.

Jesus, come to earth to do a once-and-for-ever swap, a very great exchange. Our nothing for his everything, for all the things that are in his name. Our rags for his riches… and, speaking of rags, do you see these—really filthy and tattered?

Hold up rags and place on table.

Well, they came from a leper who leapt—leapt for joy when he was healed, like the blind man did when his eyes were unsealed. Like all sinners do when Jesus is revealed. And all our rags, whatever they mean, are transformed when Jesus makes us clean.

Throw rags off table and place doll and card in their place.

Jesus, God our Emmanuel, the same yesterday, today and for ever, now shares with us God's most intimate name. I think it's the best one he's ever had. It's simply 'Abba', Dad.

Pick up the tree.

It's an awesome reminder to you and me that we belong to God's family.

Place tree and card on table.

Session Two: The sapling tree

Ten out of ten!

This piece is based on the Ten Commandments (Exodus 20:1–17), interpreting them as rules that God put in place for our benefit. Even if we find some of the rules hard to obey, the good news is that we can always get ten out of ten in God's eyes when we believe in Jesus, who came to fulfil the law (rules).

The script is written for two people to present. They could be any age, as long as they are competent, expressive readers. Alternatively, the second part could be presented using a puppet. If you really only have one person available, leave out the lines marked (opt) for 'optional'.

You will need:
A large cardboard tick, brown on one side, red on the other, initially held upside down to represent Mount Sinai; a set of number cards 1–10 plus an extra number 10 with a line underneath it

---

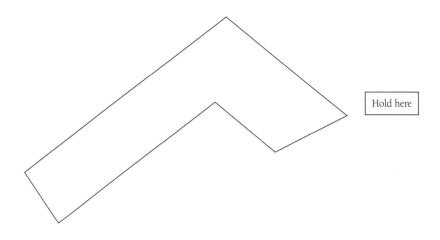

Hold here

Put the numbers 1–10 into a ringbinder file, so that they can be flipped over. The second number 10 needs to be kept by your assistant, to be held up when indicated. Teach the following responses before you begin:

- **Thunder:** Drum your feet on the ground
- **Trumpet blast:** Ta da!
- **Tremble/trembled/trembling:** Wibble wobble, wibble wobble

Hold the tick upside down, brown side visible, to represent Mount Sinai.

Person 1: Mount Sinai. The people were gathered at the foot of the mountain, waiting, waiting, waiting…

Person 2 (opt): Hang on a minute! Mountains don't have feet.

Person 1 (opt): Yes they do. Well, a foot.

Person 2 (opt): I've never seen that, a one-legged mountain. What sort of shoes do they wear?

Person 1 (opt): I don't know, but I'm sure there's a 'wide range'. Actually, the foot of the mountain is the bottom…

Person 2 (opt): Funny place for your foot, on your bottom! My foot isn't near my bottom.

Person 1 (opt): My foot might be near your bottom if you don't be quiet and let me get on with the story.

Person 1: Suddenly the people heard the loud sound of **thunder**. At the top of the mountain was a thick cloud of smoke.

Person 2 (opt): That's not very politically correct.

Person 1 (opt): What?

Person 2 (opt): Calling the smoke 'thick'! You'd get told off in school for saying something like that.

Person 1 (opt): I just mean there was a lot of it.

Person 2 (opt): Oh. That's OK, then.

Person 1: A **trumpet blast** resounded through the air, making all the people **tremble** like jellies! The ground shook; the people **trembled**. The **trumpet** sounded; the people **trembled**…

Person 2 (opt): I'm scared!

Person 1:   Think how the Israelites felt! So much smoke, rumbling **thunder**, loud **trumpet blast**, chattering teeth, knocking knees, **trembling** like jellies. Then God spoke.

Person 2 (opt): I'm surprised anyone could hear him with all that going on.

Person 1:   'I am the Lord your God who brought you out of Egypt, out of the land of slavery.'

Person 2 (opt): What? That's not nice, either.

Person 1 (opt): What now?

Person 2 (opt): Calling me an eejit! I thought God was kind.

Person 1 (opt): He is.

Person 2 (opt): Then why did he say, 'I brought you out, you eejit'?

Person 1 (opt): Out of Egypt!

Person 2 (opt): Oh, it's all this **trumpet blast**ing and **thunder**—it's made me go a bit hard of hearing. Go on, then, what else did God say?

Person 1:   Then God gave the people ten helpful rules:

(*Showing number 1*) One: good news! Don't forget, there's only one God and it's me.

(*Showing number 2*) Two: you don't need to worship anything else, because I'm the one who created everything.

(*Showing number 3*) Three: although I'm God, we're family, so I've called you by my name, the most powerful name in the whole universe. Always remember how special my name is and be careful how you use it.

(*Showing number 4*) Four: I love you to spend time with me and I know you need to take time out and relax, so I'm giving you one day every week to do just that. Let's enjoy it together.

(*Showing number 5*) Five: those who care for you in your family are very precious, so make sure you let them know how much you appreciate them. Things will be so much better if you do.

Reproduced with permission from *Let's Get Together!* by Sue Langwade (Barnabas for Children, 2013)

 www.barnabasinchurches.org.uk

(*Showing number 6*) Six: life is an amazing gift. Take good care of it, whether it's your life or someone else's.

(*Showing number 7*) Seven: I love faithfulness, so be faithful and enjoy the blessings of a lifelong marriage.

(*Showing number 8*) Eight: you can trust me to provide what you need, so you don't have to take things that belong to someone else.

(*Showing number 9*) Nine: when you tell lies, they tie you up in knots and I want you to be free, so stick to the truth.

(*Showing number 10*) Ten: don't worry, be happy! Being content with what you've got is the surest way to be happy—not always wanting more and more.

God gave the people these ten helpful rules to ensure that they stayed out of trouble and were able to live in peace and harmony with him and with one another. And to make it even better, later on he sent Jesus, who lived perfectly, not ever forgetting any one of these rules, so that if we invite him into our lives we'll always get ten out of ten (*hold underlined number ten over the other ten*). Then, when God looks at us, he sees Jesus, the perfect one—or should I say, the perfect ten.

Turn 'mountain' over to be a big tick.

Session Three: The tree bears fruit

The song of the seeds

Teach the following responses, to be used whenever the words are heard in the story.

- **Water:** make a slurping sound.
- **Goodness:** say 'yum yum'.
- **Light:** stretch upwards and say 'Whee!'
- **Air:** breathe in and sigh 'Ahh'.

Reproduced with permission from *Let's Get Together!* by Sue Langwade (Barnabas for Children, 2013)
www.barnabasinchurches.org.uk

In the orchard, the soil was rich, the soil was moist, and the soil was ready and waiting, brimful of all that a little seed needs to grow into a tree. At just the right time, the orchard planter's voice, which had once breathed the universe into life, sang the song of the seeds and they nestled down into the soil's embrace, ripe with possibilities. As their roots snaked down into the black earth, they tasted the **goodness** of the deep-down **water** and enjoyed the life-giving nutrients of the soil.

Soon all the **goodness** burst into energy inside the little seeds and pushed them up, up, up through the soil until they blinked their way into the vibrant brightness of the **light**. How they marvelled at what they saw! Trees as tall as giants (or so it seemed to them) grew around them, lush with juicy fruit of all sorts. One seed craned his neck to look up at a lemon tree.

'Your fruit is bright and yellow, like the sun. That's what I want to be—a lemon tree!' he cried.

'You may not grow up to be me,' warned the lemon tree. 'But to grow to what you're meant to be, you must:

- Drink the **water** of life…
- Soak up the **goodness** of the soil…
- Always stretch up to the **light**…
- Breathe deeply of the sweet **air**.'

'I will, I will!' declared the little seed with glee. 'And then I'll be a lemon tree!'

The seed on his left was fascinated by a sturdy, solid apple tree, covered in the tastiest-looking apples ever.

'Your fruit is green as the grass, with a fiery blush. That's what I want to be—an apple tree!'

'You may not grow up to be me,' replied the apple tree. 'But to grow to what you're meant to be, you must:

- Drink the **water** of life…
- Soak up the **goodness** of the soil…
- Always stretch up to the **light**…
- Breathe deeply of the sweet **air**.'

'I will, I will!' whooped the little seed with glee. 'And then I'll be an apple tree!'

The seed to her left couldn't take her eyes off a high, almost-to-the-sky banana tree.

'Your fruit is like a golden crescent moon. That's what I want to be—a banana tree!'

'You may not grow up to be me,' replied the banana tree. 'But to grow to what you're meant to be, you must:

- Drink the **water** of life…
- Soak up the **goodness** of the soil…
- Always stretch up to the **light**…
- Breathe deeply of the sweet **air**.'

'I will, I will!' promised the little seed with glee. 'And then I'll be a banana tree!'

Time, the rhythm of life, marched on as it does, and the seeds developed into young trees. Steadily they grew and blossomed until one day their flowers gave way to fruit—glorious fruit.

'Oh no!' shrieked the first tree. 'My fruit's all wrong! It's not bright and yellow, it's round and orange!'

'Mine's not green as the grass, it's shiny and red and tiny!' cried the second tree.

'And my fruit's not a golden crescent moon, it's purply dark!' moaned the third.

'It's not fair,' they all chanted together, shaking their roots in anger. 'We did all we were told to do! We…

- Drank the **water** of life…
- Soaked up the **goodness** of the soil…
- Always stretched up to the **light**…
- Breathed deeply of the sweet **air**.'

'And now you can see,' said the wise old trees, 'that you're each what you were meant to be—an orange tree, a cherry tree and a plum tree—because the orchard planter loves variety. Whatever fruit you produce, you'll be a deeply rooted, happy tree if you can learn to say, 'Hey! It's great to be me!'

Session Four: The tree sends out seeds

Crumbs! Did you see that?

You will need:

A beak for the storyteller (easily constructed from yellow card attached to a cap or cardboard strip); wings, simply made with strips of coloured fabric attached to sleeves; a small piece of brown wool or a sweet that looks like a worm. You will also need a lunch box, containing pre-prepared paper chains of bread and fish (see template on page 133).

This story is told from the perspective of a bird who watches the whole proceedings, so it would be helpful and attention-grabbing if the storyteller could wear the beak and wings. As you are in character as a bird, you could say a little bird told you that everyone has been thinking about how trees send out seeds so that new trees can be planted, and how we can all 'send out' things like smiles, hugs and kind words, faith or money.

If we offer those things to God, he will make them grow and grow—a sort of divine multiplication. Explain that this story is based on an event in the Bible when exactly that sort of thing happened. (You know because you were there!)

Towards the beginning of the story (as indicated), you will need to divide your audience into three groups and teach them the following responses.

- **Group one (Sun people):** They will say, 'Glare, glare, blaze, blaze' whenever the sun is mentioned.
- **Group two (Tummy people):** They will make a rumbling noise, perhaps drumming their fingers on the ground or a chair, whenever rumbling is mentioned.
- **Group three (God people):** They will shout out, 'More, more, tell us more!' when God is mentioned.

Make sure you have your lunch box handy and your 'worm' tucked away, and that you are able to easily take out the paper chains and unfold them when appropriate.

Hello there! My name's Barney and I'm an exotic bird from a tropical paradise far away. I've come all this way especially to tell you an incredible story. When you've heard it, I bet all you'll be able to say is: crumbs! Now, with all this talk of tropical paradises, you might be beginning to get a bit relaxed, so just to make sure you're still awake, I'd like you to help me with the story.

Divide the audience into groups as detailed above.

First, I must just explain that although I look young and beautiful (yes, I said young and beautiful), I'm actually very, very old. I'm so old, I remember the time when children were seen and not heard. Ah, fond memories! And I'm going to tell you a story that actually happened a long, long time ago. This particular day was a real scorcher. The **sun** was beating down so hard, you could almost hear it (in fact, I think I just did). I was perched on a branch, and underneath there was such a crowd that there wasn't even room for the dust to settle. I thought they must be giving out free tickets to [local attraction], the way people were hustling and jostling to get to the front, but, no, it seems they were all listening to this man called Jesus, who was talking to them about his father, **God**. And do you know, they hardly moved all day!

Later on, I heard a **rumbling** noise that was so scary, it made the feathers on the back of my neck stand right up. I thought it was a dinosaur approaching, and then I thought, no, they're extinct; it must be thunder. But the sky was still clear and blue. You'll never believe what it was… it was five thousand tummies **rumbling**. Everyone had been so busy listening to Jesus all day, talking about **God**, that they hadn't eaten. Five thousand people sitting there starving and not a hamburger in sight! No worms, either. Shake my tail feathers, what wouldn't I have given for a worm sandwich!

Anyway, right there, under the hot **sun**, Jesus carried right on talking to all the people, though he must have been pretty hungry himself. Shortly after that, one of his friends came up to him and said, 'Jesus, the people out there are getting thinner by the second. Listen to those tummies **rumbling**! What are we going to do?'

Just then, a little boy pushed through the crowd, carrying his lunch— five loaves and two fishes, we found out later—and he went up to Jesus and gave it to him *(hold up lunch box)*. We all said 'How sweet!' Of course, Jesus thanked him very much, and we thought he'd eat it. After all, he deserved it—he'd been doing all the talking. But no, he lifted it up to heaven and gave thanks to **God** and then started sharing it round.

Now you may think, and no one would blame you, that five loaves and two fishes wouldn't go a long way between more than five thousand people... and one bird... but what happened next was pretty strange.

Take out the paper chains and begin to unravel them. You may want to invite audience members to help you.

There seemed to be loaves and fishes everywhere!. Everybody ate their fill. In fact, they ate until they were stuffed. It was quite a sight!

And what about me, you're wondering? Well, I flew down and tucked in till I was FTB (full to bursting). There were about twelve baskets left over and I had a peck from every one. And all because that little lad shared what he had with Jesus in the first place—then Jesus had shared it (after doing a little bit of heavenly multiplication) with the rest of us! Isn't that amazing? It makes me wonder what Jesus could do with a little bit of money, a little bit of love, courage or a mustard seed of faith—or my wiggly worm. *(Show worm)* What a guy! What a **God**!

I'm sorry, I know you could listen to me all day, but I must fly now. What did I do with my packed lunch? *(Showing again)* Oh good, there it is! Cheerio!

Session Five: The tree in maturity
Trust Dad!

You will need:
Two pieces of dowel approximately 18mm in diameter × 80cm in length; a selection of cheerful pictures of dads with their children and something to attach them to when indicated in the story; a pair of large cut-out arms

---

This story is intended to be read or spoken in a traditional way, but you can help to get the attention of your audience and start them engaging their imaginations by accompanying the beginning of the story with some simple 'dowel rod' actions, as detailed below. You could prerecord or memorise the beginning of the story and use the dowel rods yourself or have an assistant who can use them while you read.

The dowel rod actions are as follows.

- 'Automatic doors': hold the rods together, parallel and vertically upright, and move them slowly apart in a smooth motion.
- 'League of friends': make large 'L'.
- 'Lift': hold both rods together, horizontally at approximately your eye level, bend your knees and move the rods slowly downwards as you straighten up.
- 'Winding corridors': hold one rod horizontally at either side of your waist and move them from side to side, as though you are 'meandering'.
- 'Painting': hold both rods vertically upright at arm's length and look admiringly at the space between them, as if looking at a painting. Alternatively, use them as paintbrush and palette.

If you go through the automatic doors of the hospital, past the League of Friends coffee bar, up in the lift, along several winding corridors displaying some interesting paintings by a local artist, you will find yourself at McKenzie Ward. This was where Sally found herself.

Put rods down. If a second person has been using the rods, they should sit quietly at the side.

Walking past Room 4b, Sally's eyes twinkled as she caught the mostly indistinct mumblings of someone muttering away to himself.

'Wish I wasn't here... it doesn't hurt that much any more... I want to go home!'

'I bet I can help,' thought Sally, peeking round the door. 'Hello! My name's Sally. What's yours?'

'I'm George,' said George, his voice sounding a little peculiar, due to some missing front teeth. He felt embarrassed but Sally didn't seem to notice at all.

'When are you having your operation, George?'

'Soon,' murmured George, the tone of his voice making it sound more like 'doom'.

'Are you worried?'

'A bit,' he shrugged, while the voice in his head shrieked, 'A very, very, very, very, very, very, very big bit!'

'Oh, you needn't be scared at all,' Sally reassured him. 'I had the same operation three days ago and now I can move around as much as I want. It's not bad at all. I've had two operations before and I was a bit nervous the first time, but look at me now—right as rain!'

'I've never had an operation,' said George.

'Well, you really shouldn't worry, because the doctor who did my operation is doing yours, and there's no way he'll let anything bad happen to you.'

'How can you be so sure?'

'Because he's the best doctor in the whole world. He's my daddy!'

With that, little Sally skipped off to the TV lounge, calling over her shoulder, 'Bye, George! See you tomorrow!'

As he thought about their brief encounter, George found himself feeling quite ashamed of all his negative thoughts. 'What a sweet child Sally is! She didn't even seem to notice that my teeth were missing because I'd had to take my dental plate out. Fancy being scared at my age, 63, when that wee child has all the confidence in the world.' Suddenly, all the fear he'd felt, all the expectations of things going wrong, all the worrying he'd done for the past few weeks, seemed to evaporate in the light of this little girl's absolute trust in her daddy.

'You know, if this doctor was prepared to do this operation on his own, much-loved child, he must be good—very good,' reasoned George, and he actually began to relax, even grabbing 40 winks before the nurse came to give him his pre-op. Later, as he drifted off into an anaesthetic-induced sleep, the theatre staff heard him murmur, 'It's OK, George, Daddy's gonna look after you!'

Begin to display pictures.

They all remarked how good it would be if those childhood days of innocence and assurance could last for ever. And the funny thing is, with our heavenly Father, they can, no matter what age we are or how many 'operations' of one sort or another we might need.

Place cut-out arms underneath the pictures.

Always underneath us are the everlasting arms of the God who truly cares. We really can trust Daddy.

Puppet sketches

These puppet sketches, which take no more than a few minutes each to present, could be performed by actors, if necessary, although puppets do have a charm all their own and are popular with all ages. You don't need a fully-fledged puppet theatre: you can create one using an inexpensive garment rail with some fabric secured over it. There are various types of puppet available that would be suitable for this purpose, the main proviso being that they need to be able to hold props or have props attached to them. This just requires a little creative imagination and some Velcro. If you do not have two suitable male puppets available, you could use animal puppets.

Pre-recorded versions of the script are available for download from www.barnabasinchurches.org.uk/extra-resources/, or you can choose the 'live' option, using the photocopiable scripts on the following pages. These, too, can be downloaded from www.barnabasinchurches.org.uk/extra-resources/.

Further downloads from the same web address include theme music to 'top and tail' the sketches and all the sound effects that are embedded in the scripts.

Each sketch is loosely based on one aspect of the session theme and can be used early in the programme to get people gathered in one place. Alongside the themes, each session also has a key word that picks up the essence of the script. Each sketch features two characters, Ted and George, who are allotment holders, and it is at the allotment that the conversations take place.

Depending on your puppets' performing space, you might like to make a suitable backdrop. You can, however, create the necessary ambience with the sound effects provided on the website mentioned above. It is probably easiest to make the required props out of cardboard or craft foam (neoprene), so that they are light enough to be attached to a puppet's hands.

Puppet pointers

Puppets should be brought on and off the stage area properly, not just 'popped up' at random. This is done by holding the arm operating the puppet straight out behind you and bringing it up to a count of four, so that it looks as if the puppet is appearing up some steps. When your puppet is up, make sure its eyes are looking at the audience and not up into outer space. Exiting is achieved by turning the puppet in towards you and bringing it down to a count of four.

A good way to practise mouth synchronisation is to have your puppet count to 20, starting from a closed mouth position, and opening the mouth on each syllable. When you have your hand in the puppet's mouth, speaking is done by moving the thumb downwards rather than the fingers upwards. Make sure you keep the mouth closed when the puppet is not speaking and the puppet's head at the correct angle. This may sound obvious but it is surprisingly easy to forget.

Go for it!

Session One: The tree is planted

Key word: Belonging

You will need:
Theme music to top and tail the sketch; sound effect of country background

---

That doesn't belong here!

Play the theme music. Ted appears, humming, then George hurries on in a panic.

George: Ted, Ted, there's something awful in my carrot patch!
Ted: Oh dear, George! What's it like?
George: It's about 15 foot long, six foot wide, and it's full of carrots, Ted.
Ted: Not your carrot patch, silly! This thing in it!
George: It's big, Ted. And it's round.
Ted: How big?
George: Big enough, Ted. And I think it might be from another world, Ted. It glows in the dark.
Ted: How do you know?
George: Well, I saw it last night and it scared the living daylights out of me.
Ted: How can it scare the living daylights out of you at night, George?

Reproduced with permission from *Let's Get Together!* by Sue Langwade (Barnabas for Children, 2013)
www.barnabasinchurches.org.uk

George:	Eh? Anyway, I was hoping it would be gone when I got back today but it's still there—bold as brass. I daren't go very close but I could see from a distance.
Ted:	It's not some strange new vegetable you've planted, is it, George? I know what you are for experimentification!
George:	No, Ted. That patch is for carrots only. It doesn't belong there. It's definitely not a carrot. And I wouldn't eat something that glows.
Ted:	Your Mabel's cooking comes pretty close sometimes, George.
George:	That's only when it's on fire, Ted.
Ted:	Which is quite often, George.
George:	Never mind that now. What am I going to do about the invader in my carrot patch?
Voice off:	Excuse me, has anybody seen my ball? Some big lads took it offa me last night and it's a new one. It's quite big and it's fluorescent.
George:	Fluo what? Is that some sort of foreign?
Ted:	No, it means it glows in the dark. Ha, ha, ha! (Calling out) I think I might know where you can find it, lad!

Ted exits momentarily, then re-enters.

George:	Be careful, Ted! You don't want to be conducted by aliens.
Ted:	Right, George, I think you'll be safe to get back to your carrots now. They might not make you glow in the dark but, if my mother were right, they might just help you see in the dark.
George:	And grow hairs on your chest, Ted.
Ted:	Better not tell that to your Mabel, George!

Both exit. Play the theme music.

Reproduced with permission from *Let's Get Together!* by Sue Langwade (Barnabas for Children, 2013)
www.barnabasinchurches.org.uk

Session Two: The sapling tree

Key word: Protection

You will need:
A pointy carrot; theme music to top and tail the sketch; sound effects of country background

George, the great protector

Play the theme music. George is marching up and down, holding a large, pointy-looking carrot. Ted enters.

George:	Hup, two, three, four; hup, two, three, four…
Ted:	Morning, George!
George:	Halt! Who goes there, friend or foe?
Ted:	What are you talking about, you numpty? It's me, Ted. I'm your friend, of course.
George:	Aha! That's what you say! But how do I know you're really who you say you are?
Ted:	Because you can see me, clear as day.
George:	You could just be a horrible illusion sent to taunt me.
Ted:	Horrible illusion? Well, thank you very much. I'm not sure I am your friend now.
George:	Aha! See, I told you.
Ted:	Listen, how about I tell you this: you're wearing your Superman undies.
George:	Fizzling fertiliser! How do you know that?
Ted:	Because I'm your friend, of course! And I know that you always wear your Superman undies on this day of the week.
George:	All right, I believe you.
Ted:	Thank goodness for that. So what's all this about, then, George?

Reproduced with permission from *Let's Get Together!* by Sue Langwade (Barnabas for Children, 2013)
www.barnabasinchurches.org.uk

George: I've just bought a new tree for my allotment, Ted, and they told me I've got to be sure and protect it from harmful predators. They said fencing might help. Well, as I don't have one of those skinny little swords they do fencing with, I thought I'd use this nice pointy carrot and that would do the trick. It's a bit scary, eh?

Ted: I'm not sure it's the carrot that's scary, George. But, er, George, I think they probably meant you should put a little fence round the base of your tree to stop foxes or dogs or anything else getting at your tree and doing it harm. You put the fencing in place and then it protects your tree while it's growing.

George: So I don't have to be on patrol all the time? Phew! I was wondering how I was going to explain that to Mabel and stay awake for the next few months.

Ted: Look, why don't we go together and buy something to put round your tree? Then maybe we can pop over to the Dog and Duck. We'll stop off at Neddy's field on the way and you can give him that carrot. There's no 'point' in you keeping it! Ha, ha, ha!

Both exit. Play the theme music.

Reproduced with permission from *Let's Get Together!* by Sue Langwade (Barnabas for Children, 2013)

 www.barnabasinchurches.org.uk

Session Three: The tree bears fruit

Key word: Variety

You will need:
Tree catalogue; theme music to top and tail the sketch; sound effects of country background

---

Variety is the spice of life!

Play the theme music. George is holding an open catalogue and reading it. Ted enters.

Ted:	What's that you've got there, George?
George:	It's a tree catalogue, Ted.
Ted:	Oh, what kind of tree are you wanting to buy now, George?
George:	Ah, now that would be telling, Ted.
Ted:	Exactly. That's why I'm asking, George.
George:	It's to be a surprise for Mabel's birthday, Ted. I think she'll really like it. Trouble is, I just can't find anyone who sells what I want.
Ted:	I didn't think your Mabel was very keen on gardening, George. I thought that's why you took it up.
George:	Oh, she's not, but this would be something she'd use every Christmas, Ted.
Ted:	Oh, a Christmas tree! Are you going to grow her her own? That's a nice idea, George.
George:	Not a Christmas tree, silly! Whatever made you think that? No! A fruit salad tree. That's what I want, a fruit salad tree. You see, she makes a lovely fruit salad trifle every Christmas, and I thought being able to pick it off her own tree would be really novel.
Ted:	Very novel indeed, George!
George:	Trouble is, as I say, I haven't been able to find one anywhere.

Reproduced with permission from *Let's Get Together!* by Sue Langwade (Barnabas for Children, 2013)
www.barnabasinchurches.org.uk

Ted: Er... I think you'll find that's because they don't exist, George.

George: What? Are you sure, Ted?

Ted: I am. All the fruit comes from different trees, George, and then they mix it all together to make a fruit salad.

George: Oh, that seems a bit messy, Ted. I think it would have been a lot easier if someone had designed a fruit salad tree.

Ted: Maybe so, George, but that way you wouldn't get all the variety. Everybody's fruit salad would be the same, whereas now you can get loads of variety by mixing up the fruit any way you want.

George: Aye, I suppose.

Ted: Why don't we go down to the market, and you can buy Mabel a case of tinned fruit salad—the one with the glacé cherries in, so it's really posh. She'll like that.

George: Oh yes, good idea, Ted, and I'll get some runner beans while I'm there.

Ted: Why's that, George? You're not thinking of having a bean marathon?

George: Don't be daft! What do you think I am, an idiot?

Both exit. Play the theme music.

Reproduced with permission from *Let's Get Together!* by Sue Langwade (Barnabas for Children, 2013)
www.barnabasinchurches.org.uk

Session Four: The tree sends out seeds

Key word: Multiplying

You will need:
Large marrow; toy kitten; theme music to top and tail the sketch; sound effects of country background. There will also need to be something to put the marrow on when George puts it down. This could be done by moving Ted to face the back, blocking the audience's view of George and the marrow while it is moved from George's hands on to a ledge or table of some sort.

Multiplying marrows

Ted is standing at one side of the puppet theatre. George enters, carrying a giant marrow. Play the theme music.

George: Here, Ted, give us a hand with this monster, will you? My knees are about to give way.

They put the marrow down.

Ted: Galloping gooseberries, George! Where on earth did you get a whopping great thing like that? It hasn't been talking to you in a deep voice, has it? Saying, 'Feed me, George!' Or anything strange like that? Or maybe you've been talking to it and it's full of hot air.

George: Course not! Vegetables don't talk, Ted. Anyway, I didn't grow it, Fred did. And he gave it to me.

Ted: Why's that, then, George? Did he think you needed feeding up or summat? Hey! You know, if you put some wheels on that and a tow bar, we could tow it to Yarmouth and camp out in it for a week. Or we could take it out as a marrow boat on the canals.

George: Some time ago, Ted, I gave Fred a packet of seeds I had going spare. I didn't have any more room on my plot and I knew Fred did, so I gave them to him, and look what he did with them! Grew a whopping great load of marrows and he's very kindly sharing them with his friends.

Ted: I hope they're not all as big as that one, George, or they'll be taking over the village. 'Invasion of the Marrow Monsters.' We'd all be stuffed.

George: No! It's the marrows that'd be stuffed, Ted. Ha, ha! Anyway, I have got something in mind for this—after we've enjoyed some mashed marrow, that is. I'm going to scoop it clean and make a little playhouse for Rover.

Ted: Rover? I didn't think you had a dog, George. I thought Mabel was allergic.

George: That's right, Ted. Oh, here's Rover now.

Exits and brings on a little kitten.

Ted: That's very sweet, George, but isn't Rover a strange name for a cat?

George: A bit unusual, I'll grant you, Ted. But it was something our Mabel said when she found him swinging from the curtains that made me think of it.

Ted: I would have thought you'd have called him Tarzan in that case.

George: No, Ted, Mabel said he was just like me—barking mad— so I thought Rover would suit him down to the ground. Come on, we've got some cooking to do.

Both exit. Play the theme music.

Session Five: The tree in maturity

Key word: Shelter

You will need:
Toy kitten; theme music to top and tail the sketch; sound effects of country background; sound effects of thunder, whistling kettle and rain

---

Shelter in the storm

Play the theme music. Ted and George enter together.

Ted: Well, George, this looks set to be the perfect day.

George: You're not wrong there, Ted. Mabel's gone to her sister's, cat's been fed, everything here's weeded and watered, kettle's on. Perfick!

Ted: Would you like a biscuit, George? There's fig newtons, garibaldis, pink wafers, chocolate digestives, jammy dodgers...

George: Yes, please, Ted.

Ted: Well, which, George?

George: Oh, I can't remember them all, Ted. Tell me again.

Ted: I'll just do a lucky dip, George, or the kettle will have boiled dry.

Thunder sound effects.

George: Oo er! What was that, Ted? I thought the forecast for today was OK.

Ted: It was, George, but you know what storms are like. It's as if they have a mind of their own. I'm sure they enjoy popping up unexpected wherever they please and taking us by surprise.

Thunder is heard even louder.

George: Ooo! I don't like it, Ted! Reminds me of my Mabel thundering down the stairs like a herd of elephants when I forget and leave the toilet seat up. Very scary!

Ted: I imagine it would be, George. I'll tell you what, why don't we shelter inside my little hut to have our tea? It's completely rainproof and very cosy. We can have a game or two of cards to take your mind off the storm. It'll soon pass.

George: That sounds like a very good idea, Ted.

Thunder is heard even louder.

Ted: Oh, it's getting closer. Like as not, it'll rain in a bit. Come on, you don't want to end up like a wet line of washing.

George: Certainly not this week's washing, Ted! Mabel decided to wash all her smalls this week. Not that they're all that small, truth be told, Ted.

Ted: T.m.i, George, as the young folk say. T.m.i!

George: T.m.i? Is that what they call their smalls nowadays? I thought it was tongs or summat.

Ted: T.m.i means 'too much information', George.

Sound effect of kettle whistling

Ted: 'ere… saved by the whistle!

Sound effect of rain.

Ted: And here comes the rain! Let's get under cover, George. We'll be as snug as a bug in a rug.

George: Funnily enough, I once found a bug in a rug…

Ted: *(Dragging him off)* George!

George: *(Off stage)* You're almost as bad as Mabel. *(Pause)* Oh, thank you. Jammy dodgers are my favourite, you know.

Play the theme music.

Reproduced with permission from *Let's Get Together!* by Sue Langwade (Barnabas for Children, 2013)

 www.barnabasinchurches.org.uk

Serial drama

This series of short dramas revolves around the antics of the Wood family, a motley collection of characters including a talking dog—so not altogether your average family set-up. However, there are elements that I'm sure will be familiar to most people, such as Woody, the monosyllabic teenager, and Auntie May de Wood, the slightly eccentric relation. Each episode touches lightly on the session theme, expressing an aspect of it in the context of the Wood family's day-to-day life. The dramas are meant to be fun and something that people of all ages can enjoy together.

Each script could stand alone, although there is a sequential thread if you intend to perform more than one of the episodes. As they are not serious dramatic pieces, the characters could be played by any age and either gender, provided it is done with lots of confidence and a huge sense of fun.

The theme can be expanded at home afterwards, using the take-home resource 'Bible bloodhound', in which Chip the dog has sniffed out some Bible verses for families to look up at home, to explore parallels between them and the scene that has been played out.

The photocopiable scripts are also available as a download from www.barnabasinchurches.org.uk/extra-resources/, as is the theme music (which you might like to use to top and tail each episode), Chip's song in Episode 2, a backing track for the sequence in Episode 3, and all the sound effects mentioned in the text.

Cast of characters
- Mrs Wood: The mum of the Wood family
- Grandpa Wood: A crossword fanatic
- Woody Wood: The older son, a barely intelligible teenager, who needs to have a wide repertoire of meaningful grunts
- Teresa Wood: Woody's charming younger sibling, who has an uncanny ability to interpret Woody's grunts
- Auntie May: An eccentric aunt who spouts (her own) bad poetry and whose knitting is even 'verse'

- Chip: The Wood family's talking dog—a chirpy, cheeky sort.
- (*Episode five only*) Aquaman: An athletic superhero type (an ideal part for your local vicar)
- Water wafters: To waft fabric

Costume suggestions
- Mum: 'Mumsy' outfit, nothing too trendy
- Grandpa: Older gent's clothes, perhaps with the addition of an overall for Episode 3. Snorkel, flippers, cap and towel for Episode 5
- Woody: Teenage outfit
- Teresa: Little girlish outfit, perhaps with hair in bunches, flat shoes and ankle socks
- Auntie May: Eccentric, arty look
- Chip: The best dog costume you can get hold of
- Aquaman: Superhero garb, with the essential pants over tights

Props list
- Headphones for Woody
- Crazy foam ice creams
- Small table and chairs for Wood family lounge
- Deckchairs and beach paraphernalia
- Telephone (mobile or landline)
- Sundry items for kennel (cuddly toy and so on)
- Knitting for Auntie May
- Cards saying 'Muttz 4 U'; Two days later; Ahh!
- Newspaper and pen for Grandpa
- Design for kennel (cardboard)
- Large bone

Episode 1: Day of the dog

Key words: Rescue, belonging

The scene should suggest the Wood family lounge, with a couple of chairs and a table, and perhaps a few knick-knacks to make the scene look more homely. Woody and Grandpa are sitting down, Grandpa immersed in a crossword and Woody with headphones on, nodding to music and occasionally singing out the odd incomprehensible phrase. Mrs Wood is on the phone (could be landline or mobile) and Teresa and Auntie May are standing near her, obviously very excited. Auntie May is knitting a long, thin, multicoloured item, which we later learn is a dog's lead. They get into place and freeze until the 'Voice off' is finished.

Play the theme music.

Voice off:	This is the Wood family. They live in the Tree House, Forest Lane, Twigenham. There's Teresa Wood, Woody Wood, Grandpa Wood, Mrs Wood and Auntie May de Wood (from a slightly eccentric branch of the family). Today the Wood family are excited because they've been hoping to get a dog, and now it seems there's one that is just right for them…
Mrs Wood:	Yes! Yes! Thank you! Goodbye! At last! Muttz 4 U think they've found the perfect dog for us. He's very well behaved; very, very cute and very, very, very clever. When they asked him if he'd like to come and live with us, he barked twice for yes. *(Teresa and Auntie May do an 'I'm excited' dance)* They asked, would we like to go and meet him today? What do you think?
Woody:	*(Taking off headphones)* Grunt
Teresa:	Oh yes, Woody said he'd love to, and I would, too.
Mrs Wood:	How about you, Grandpa? Will you come with us?
Grandpa:	Hmmm, what? What's a six-letter word that can be a tooth, a four-legged pet or a character in Doctor Who?

Reproduced with permission from *Let's Get Together!* by Sue Langwade (Barnabas for Children, 2013)
www.barnabasinchurches.org.uk

All think, then shake their heads.

Teresa: I'm not sure. *(Indicating audience)* Maybe these nice people could help you, Grandpa.

Grandpa repeats clue and, hopefully, the audience will respond with 'canine'.

Mrs Wood: Thank goodness we've got intelligent people here. Hey! Canine! Of course! It's another way of saying 'dog'. I think it's a sign.

Teresa: Yay! I can't wait! A fluffy, furry, funny, faithful friend! Isn't that fab, Woody?

Woody: Grunt

Teresa: I'm so glad you think so, too.

Auntie May: I think I feel a poem coming on.

There once was a doggy with no place to call his own
So the Wood family came and took him to their home.
'Woof, Woof,' he cried as they called out his name.
He'd never have to sleep in a lonely kennel again.

(Sobs) Oh, that's so beautiful, even though I say so myself.

Mrs Wood: That's a point—his name. What are we going to call him? Maybe he already has a name. Maybe we should let him choose.

Grandpa: Maybe we should go and see what he's like first. *(Holding up newspaper)* I'll bring this with me and you can all help me do it on the way.

Teresa: I suppose it's better than playing alphabet lists. We never did think of a superhero beginning with 'q', did we?

Woody: Grunt

Teresa: Of course you can sit by the window, Woody.

They all exit and furniture is removed or pushed back.

Reproduced with permission from *Let's Get Together!* by Sue Langwade (Barnabas for Children, 2013)

          www.barnabasinchurches.org.uk

Scene 2 is set in the kennels. There is a 'Muttz 4 U' sign hanging, or a card could be held up. Chip is walking up and down excitedly.

Chip: Hello, everyone! Can you keep a secret? I can talk. You won't tell anyone, will you? Good. Oooh, I'm so excited! I hear they might have found a family for me. I wonder what they're like. I hope they're kind and fun and have plenty of food. I like my food. Sausages are my favourite. Has anybody got a sausage? Or a bit of cheese? I thought I could smell cheese, but maybe it's just cheesy feet. I'll do anything for a bit of mature Cheddar. I've got some really good tricks I can do, but I'll save those for later.

   I've been quite lonely, you know. *('Ahh' card is held up)* My best friend, Flearoy, went to a new home. He was a real joker, Flearoy was. He said, 'You scratch my back and I'll scratch yours.' I said, 'Do you have a problem with fleas?' He said, 'No, all my fleas are very well trained, thank you.' Ha, ha… Oh, maybe you have to be a dog to appreciate that one. *(Noises off)* Here they come! Better put my best cute pose on.

The Wood family wander on and are all suitably impressed by Chip. Grandpa is still doing his crossword and Auntie May is knitting. With a bit of artistic licence, Chip can interact subtly with the audience without the family noticing.

Teresa: *(Stroking him)* Hello doggy! Oh, you're so cute! *(Chip turns and winks at the audience)* We've brought you a sausage.

Mrs Wood: And a bit of cheese. I hope you don't mind mature Cheddar—it's our favourite.

Auntie May: I'm knitting you a lovely long lead. In all the colours of the rainbow.

Reproduced with permission from *Let's Get Together!* by Sue Langwade (Barnabas for Children, 2013)
www.barnabasinchurches.org.uk

Chip, looking somewhat dismayed, howls.

Auntie May: Oh, you sing, too. What a talented doggie! Maybe we can do a duet.

She howls and Chip looks at her as if she's mad.

Grandpa: Quiet, everyone! Only two more to go... What's a five-letter word meaning 'not smooth'?

Chip: Ruff!

Grandpa: Rough! That's it. What a clever dog!

Mrs Wood: What are we going to call you? I see they've called you Bluebell for now, after the place they found you—Bluebell Wood. Hmmm...

Chip: *(To audience)* I hope they change that. I've been the laughing stock of the kennels.

Mrs Wood: *(To audience)* These people seem to be very clever. Let's ask them. Do you think he suits that name?

Audience: *(With encouragement from Chip, unseen by the Woods, of course)* No!

Woody: Grunt

Teresa: Hey, Woody, that's not a bad idea. Woody says, 'What about Chip?' I like it.

Chip: *(Giving thumbs up)* Woof, woof! *(To audience)* Chip off the old block. I like it. Or Chip, short for chipolata—even better!

Mrs Wood: What do you think, Grandpa?

Grandpa: Last one! Seven-letter word meaning 'just right'...

Together: Perfect!

Mrs Wood: Well, Chip. It looks like you belong to the Wood family now. I hope that's OK?

Chip: *(As they exit)* OK? It's doggone marvellous!

Play the theme music.

Reproduced with permission from *Let's Get Together!* by Sue Langwade (Barnabas for Children, 2013)

 www.barnabasinchurches.org.uk

Episode 2: New dog, old tricks

Key words: Training, obedience

The scene is the Wood family lounge. Play the theme music.

Voice off: This is the home of the Wood family. They live in the Tree House, Forest Lane, Twigenham. There's Teresa Wood, Woody Wood, Grandpa Wood, Mrs Wood and Auntie May de Wood (from a slightly eccentric branch of the family). They have recently adopted a dog called Chip and today they are going to begin his training.

Chip enters, yawning and stretching.

Chip: Morning, everyone! It was so good to sleep in my very own, brand new bed. I slept like a dog. Well, first things first. I am a properly house-trained dog, so, if you'll excuse me, I'll just go and find a suitable spot to you know what…

Chip exits.

Teresa: *(Enters, skipping)* Chip! Chip, Chip. Chippy! Oh, where's Chip? I hope he hasn't run away. Has anybody seen him? *(She responds appropriately to any replies)* I've got lots of sausages for his breakfast—he seemed to like those. I'm going to start his training today. He'll have to learn some manners. We need to make sure he'll do as he's told in case he's ever in danger. I think he'll learn really quickly—he seems like a very clever boy. I'll go and get the sausages so that we can start as soon as he comes back.

Teresa exits.

Reproduced with permission from *Let's Get Together!* by Sue Langwade (Barnabas for Children, 2013)
www.barnabasinchurches.org.uk

Chip: (*Enters*) Ah, that's better. Right! I wonder what's planned
               for today. I expect they'll want to train me. That's great 'cos
               it usually means lots of treats. I'll pretend I don't know
               how to do anything yet, and they'll be so pleased when
               they think they've taught me, they'll give me yummy stuff
               to eat. Do you want to know something? I used to be on
               the stage. Watch this! Say, 'Beg.' (*Audience obeys and Chip
               does some very dramatic ham acting*) 'Please, Sir, can I have
               some more?' Or how about this? 'I beg you, don't hurt me,
               please don't hurt me! I'm allergic to pain!' And when it
               comes to 'Sit!' I can do a casual sit, formal sit, flirty sit...
               A dog for all seasons, that's me. (*Demonstrates sitting, using
               one of the chairs*)

*Chip sings his song. If you have lots of budding thespians, you might like to have
extra dogs who come on as backing singers to sing the chorus, saying 'He' instead
of 'I'. The music can be downloaded from www.barnabasinchurches.org.uk/extra-
resources/.*

Chip: (*Chorus*) My name's Chip. I'm a clever dog.
               I do tricks like falling off a log.
               I 'sit' and 'stand' and 'beg', and then
               While they train me, I train them!

               (*Verse 1*) If no one will play with me;
               if they'd rather watch TV,
               I roll around and show my tum.
               Then it's tickle time... Oh what fun!

               (*Sing Chorus, then verse 2*) When they need some exercise
               I get my lead and roll my eyes.
               I pull a face and wave my paw.
               Then 'Hey presto!' we're out that door.

www.barnabasinchurches.org.uk

(*Sing Chorus, then verse 3*) When it's time for me to eat,
I let them give me lots of treats.
I smile my smile and wag my tail.
Then I get bones—it never fails.

(*Chorus*) My name's Chip. I'm a clever dog.
I do tricks like falling off a log.
I 'sit' and 'stand' and 'beg', and then
While they train me, I train them!

Teresa, Auntie May and Woody enter.

Teresa: Come on, Woody and Auntie May. You can help me train Chip. What shall we do first, Woody?
Woody: Grunt
Teresa: Excellent idea! We'll teach him to sit. OK, Chip. Sit! (*Chip looks puzzled*) Sit, Chip! I think we'd better show him. Look at Woody and Auntie May, Chip. Woody, sit! (*He does, dog-style*) Auntie May, sit! (*Ditto*) Chip, sit! (*He still looks puzzled*) Watch me, Chip. (*Very slowly*) S… i… t! (*Teresa sits*)

All characters are sitting in a row, facing the audience. Behind them, Chip does his different types of sitting on the chair.

Auntie May: (*Getting up*) It's no good. Perhaps he will respond better to an artistic approach. I feel a poem coming on.

A dog must learn the rules,
we don't mean to be cruel,
just teach you a few laws
so you don't harm your paws.
A dog who can sit and fetch and stay
will live to fight another day!

> We humans have so much brain,
> it's only fair that we should train
> a dog to beg or not to beg,
> that is the question!

Chip   (*To audience*) I can't stand any more of this. Time to do my bit and sit.

Chip walks to the front and sits.

Teresa: Oh, you clever Chip. You're sitting. Have a sausage! (*He winks at audience*) Isn't he clever, Woody?
Woody: Grunt
Teresa: I think so too, Woody. He does deserve another bit of sausage. Let's go and tell Mum and Grandpa.

They exit. Chip's music plays and he goes off dancing.

Episode 3: To the dog house
Key words: Working together

The scene is the Wood family garden. A clear stage would be fine, with a short burst of the country sound effects from the puppet sketches. NB: If the drama is to be performed as a one-off, use the additional material on page 130.

Play the theme music.

Voice off: This is the Wood family garden. The Wood family live in the Tree House, Forest Lane, Twigenham. There's Teresa Wood, Woody Wood, Grandpa Wood, Mrs Wood and Auntie May de Wood (from a slightly eccentric branch of the family) and their new dog, Chip. Today they are going to build Chip a kennel.

Reproduced with permission from *Let's Get Together!* by Sue Langwade (Barnabas for Children, 2013)

 www.barnabasinchurches.org.uk

Chip enters and sits on the side of the stage. All the family enter, dressed for some DIY. Teresa is carrying a design for a luxury kennel.

Teresa:	Look, Chip, me and Woody have designed a kennel just for you, haven't we, Woody?
Woody:	Grunt
Teresa:	That's right, Woody, so that Chip can have a bit of peace and quiet if he wants.
Chip:	*(Aside)* Especially when Auntie May starts on one of her poems. Grrruff!
Grandpa:	I've been out and bought everything we'll need: wood for me, glue for Woody, paint for Teresa, fabric for Mum and paper and pen for Auntie May.
Chip:	*(To audience)* Paper and pen? What's she going to use them for? Oh no! Are you thinking what I'm thinking? More bad poetry! Yucky doodle do!
Mrs Wood:	I'm going to make you some lovely curtains, Chip, so you can have a bit of privacy.
Teresa:	We're all going to work together to get it done as quickly as possible.

They get into a line across the stage, from stage right to stage left: Grandpa, Woody, Auntie May, Mrs Wood, and Teresa. The following routine is based on an old music hall standard, 'If I were not upon the stage', which relies on good timing. That means you have to duck in time to avoid being hit by the person next to you doing their action. Each person steps forward to perform their sequence, then steps back, stepping forward again to add themselves into the next person's sequence as the piece builds up. Grandpa is sawing wood, Woody is brushing glue up and down the length of wood, Auntie May is being dramatic, Mrs Wood is sewing large stitches, and Teresa is painting. All will become clear as you work it through, but you can find an example of the sequence on YouTube if you get stuck (entitled 'We built a kennel': see www.youtube.com/watch?v=uJKDhvroVfw&feature=plcp).

Reproduced with permission from *Let's Get Together!* by Sue Langwade (Barnabas for Children, 2013)
www.barnabasinchurches.org.uk

Play the backing track loop.

All: We're going to build a kennel and we'll make it out of wood,
            So let's all work together to make sure it's really good.
Grandpa: (*Stepping forward*) Two by four, get busy with the saw (*repeat*).

'Two': one arm up, one down; 'Four': both arms out to the side; 'Busy': both forward for sawing action. Grandpa steps back into line.

All: We're going to build a kennel and we'll make it out of wood,
            So let's all work together to make sure it's really good.
Woody: (Steps forward and grunts rhythmically)

He should be saying, 'Glue up, glue down, brush has got stuck' twice; perhaps Teresa could articulate the lines for him. 'Up': brush up; 'Down': brush down; 'Stuck': try to get up but stay down as though stuck.

After Woody has done his actions twice through, Grandpa joins in and does his own sequence twice. Both then step back.

All: We're going to build a kennel and we'll make it out of wood,
            So let's all work together to make sure it's really good.
Auntie May: Thank you all, thank you all, so glad you like my poem (*repeat*).

'Thank': hands clasped to left shoulder; 'Thank': hands clasped to right shoulder; 'Glad': fling both arms out to side.

After Auntie May has done her actions twice through, Woody and Grandpa join in, doing their sequences twice. All step back.

All: We're going to build a kennel and we'll make it out of wood,
            So let's all work together to make sure it's really good.

Reproduced with permission from *Let's Get Together!* by Sue Langwade (Barnabas for Children, 2013)
 www.barnabasinchurches.org.uk

Mrs Wood: One stitch, two stitch… Oops, the needle's dropped (*repeat*).

'One': exaggerated sewing action; 'Two': sewing action; 'Oops': bend down.

After Mrs Wood has done her actions twice through, Auntie May, Woody and Grandpa join in, doing their sequences twice, keeping the routine going. At end, all step back.

All: We're going to build a kennel and we'll make it out of wood,
So let's all work together to make sure it's really good.

Teresa: Dip the brush, stir the paint, slap it on the wall! (*repeat*)

'Dip': bend down, right arm in pot; 'Stir': stay down, stirring; 'Slap': stand, right arm out to side.

After Teresa has done her sequence twice, the others join in as before.

All: We've built a lovely kennel and we've made it out of wood,
We all worked together so it should be really good.

Mrs Wood: Close your eyes, Chip! That's coming along really nicely.

A kennel appears behind them. It needs to be big enough for Chip to fit inside.

Mrs Wood: Just a few finishing touches. Come on, everybody, bring the last bits.

They hang a pair of curtains, put up a sign saying 'Chip's pad' and maybe add a cuddly toy, bone and such like. You might like to play the downloadable 'busy music' soundtrack while all this happens.

Chip: I can't wait to see. This is very special. No one's ever made me a kennel before.

Teresa: OK, Chip, open your eyes!

Reproduced with permission from *Let's Get Together!* by Sue Langwade (Barnabas for Children, 2013)
www.barnabasinchurches.org.uk

Chip opens his eyes. Sound effect of a trumpet as they reveal the kennel.

Auntie May: This is definitely an occasion which should be marked with a poem.

Chip: I know what mark her poems would get from me.

Chip gets into kennel and shuts the door.

Auntie May: *(As she's being dragged off)* Woof for the kennel!
Woof, woof, woof!
Woof for the kennel, woof, woof, woo...

Play the theme music.

Episode 4: Dem bones, dem bones, dem dry bones
Key words: Sharing, sacrifice

The scene is the Wood family lounge. Grandpa is busy with a crossword, Woody has his headphones on, and Teresa is practising her ballet moves. Chip enters, carrying a large bone. He stands at the side of the stage and, once voice off has finished, addresses the audience.

Play the theme music.

Voice off: This is the Wood family. They live in the Tree House, Forest Lane, Twigenham. There's Teresa Wood, Woody Wood, Grandpa Wood, Mrs Wood, Auntie May de Wood (from a slightly eccentric branch of the family) and their cute dog, Chip. Chip has been out exploring...

Chip: Hello, everyone. Look what I found! Isn't that the biggest, most beautiful bone you've ever seen? I was digging in the field round the back, and there it was. I'm so excited. I'll

Reproduced with permission from *Let's Get Together!* by Sue Langwade (Barnabas for Children, 2013)
 www.barnabasinchurches.org.uk

	put it in my kennel, and then I can put my paws up later, and me and my bone can enjoy a long evening together, reading the Barking Gazette.
Mrs Wood:	(Enters, carrying an opened letter) Oh no! This is dreadful! Whatever are we going to do?
Teresa:	Mum! What's happened?
Mrs Wood:	They're going to build a big new motorway and it's going to go right through our house. This is a compulsory purchase order. We have to sell our lovely home and move. This is terrible!

Sound effect to denote an awful moment.

Grandpa:	Let me see.
Woody:	Grunt
Teresa:	No, I don't want to move either, Woody. This house is perfect for us.
Mrs Wood:	We'll never find another house big enough for all of us for the money they're offering. It's criminal! We might not have room for Auntie May.
Chip:	(To audience) Every cloud has a silver lining.
Auntie May:	(Entering) What's this? Are they forcing us out of our familial home? I feel a stirring in my very soul.
Chip:	I feel a stirring, but it's not in my soul. Oh no, here we go again. (He puts his paws over his ears)
Auntie May:	Woe, woe and thrice woe! A family with nowhere to go, Thrust from the bosom of our home, The lonely streets to roam, to roam, to roam…
Chip:	(Aside) I wish she'd go to Rome. Seriously, they all look so sad. I wish there was something I could do. I know—it'll be a big sacrifice, but it's worth it. I'll cheer Mrs Wood up

Reproduced with permission from *Let's Get Together!* by Sue Langwade (Barnabas for Children, 2013)
www.barnabasinchurches.org.uk

by giving her my bone. It's not much, I know, but it's the best thing I've got.

Chip takes the bone and offers it to Mrs Wood.

Mrs Wood:	Thank you, Chip. I know you're trying to help. That's so kind.
Teresa:	*(Giving him a hug)* Oh Chip, you're such a good dog. I hope we can find a new home with a nice garden, so you can stay with us.
Grandpa:	*(Taking the bone)* Could I have a look at that? Be back in a moment…
Woody:	Grunt
Teresa:	You're right, Woody. Why do we need another motorway?
Grandpa:	*(Holding up newspaper)* Look at this!
Mrs Wood:	We haven't got time for crosswords right now, Grandpa.
Grandpa:	No! Look! What a coincidence! *(All freeze momentarily looking askance at audience)* There's an article in here about ancient ruins, and the bones in the pictures look just like Chip's bone. Where did you find it, Chip, old boy? Show us where you dug it up. Bring a spade, everyone! Follow Chip!

Play the 'busy music' soundtrack. They run round the stage with Chip directing the way. They all copy what he does, even scratching his ear and so on. Eventually they all exit. Show a card saying, 'Two days later'. They all re-enter.

Grandpa:	Good old Chip! He saved the day.
Teresa:	He gave us his very best treasure, not realising that that's exactly what it was—buried treasure.
Mrs Wood:	Now that they've found all those other ancient artefacts in the field, they're going to have to build the motorway somewhere else.

Reproduced with permission from *Let's Get Together!* by Sue Langwade (Barnabas for Children, 2013)

 www.barnabasinchurches.org.uk

Teresa:	Three cheers for Chip! Hip, hip, hooray…
Auntie May:	Hip, hip for Chip,
	Hip, hip hooray!
	Our hero dog
	Who saved the day!
	Without a moan
	He gave his bone…
Chip:	… and now we can stay in our lovely home.
All:	Chip!
Teresa:	You can talk!
Chip:	(Putting his paw over his mouth) Oops!

Play the theme music.

Episode 5: Ruff seas

Key words: Protection, rescue

Play seaside sound effects to denote that the scene is at the beach. There will need to be at least one length of blue fabric at the back of the stage, which will represent the waves later. Have a few shells scattered around at the back.

Voice off:	This is the Wood family. They live in the Tree House, Forest Lane, Twigenham. There's Teresa Wood, Woody Wood, Grandpa Wood, Mrs Wood, Auntie May de Wood (from a slightly eccentric branch of the family) and their cute talking dog, Chip. Grandpa Wood has won a crossword competition and the prize is a family day out at the new, amazing seaside theme park, Beachquest.

All except Grandpa enter with bags, deckchairs, shades, knotted hankies and so on. Auntie May is carrying some knitting. Chip has trouble putting up his deckchair but manages after a struggle.

Voice off:	Good morning and welcome to Beachquest! We're sure you'll enjoy all the wonderful facilities we have here. Even our sea is a comfortable 70 degrees. Remember, if you get too much sand in your 'sand'wich, not to worry—there are several tasty cafés where you can eat your fill. Have a nice day!
Chip:	(Settling down into a chair) Ah! This is the life! A good book (1001 Whiffiest Sniffs), my favourite DVD for later (Bonio and Juliet), and a bag of pork scratchings.
Teresa:	I'm going to go for a paddle. And I'll pick up some shells for my collection. They've got some fabulous shells here.
Woody:	Grunt
Teresa:	OK, Woody, I'll bring you one back!

Teresa moves to the back of the stage.

Auntie May:	What a pleasant smell rises up my nose!
	Much nicer than a fragrant rose.
	How I love the sand and sea-fresh air
	blowing through my gorgeous hair!
	There's only one thing that can spoil it:
	You can never find a nearby toilet!
Mrs Wood:	Come on, Auntie May, let's go and get ice creams. Look after our things, Chip.
Chip:	(Yawns) I'm so sleepy suddenly! (To audience) If you see anything odd, can you shout and wake me up? Thanks! ZZzzzzz...

Play scary music. Grandpa comes on in snorkel and flippers, with a cap on backwards and a large towel draped round him. He is walking rather strangely. Hopefully the audience will shout out; if not, Chip should just wake up of his own accord.

Reproduced with permission from *Let's Get Together!* by Sue Langwade (Barnabas for Children, 2013)

 www.barnabasinchurches.org.uk

Chip:	What? Argh! What's that? Is it the beast from the deep?
Grandpa:	No, silly, it's me, Grandpa. I fancied doing a bit of snorkelling. Where is everyone?

At the back of the stage, the blue fabric is wafted higher in the air.

Teresa:	Oh no! My best shell is floating away. Let me see if I can reach it…

She becomes overwhelmed by the 'waves'.

Teresa:	Oh, help, I can't swim!
Chip:	Oh dear, I can only doggy-paddle and I'm really slow.
Grandpa:	I can hardly move in this stuff. Woody! Woody!

Mrs Wood comes back with ice creams (crazy foam). At that moment, Woody jumps up and knocks them in her face.

Mrs Wood:	*(Wandering blindly about)* Where am I?
Auntie May:	I haven't quite finished knitting my swimming costume. Oh dear. Oh dear! What rhymes with 'drowning'?

They all run around aimlessly for a couple of seconds, panicking. Then all freeze.

Voice off:	This looks bad! Is this the end for the Wood family as we know it? Can anyone save Teresa?
Aquaman:	*(Entering and posing front of stage)* Stand back, everyone! This is a job for Aquaman.

Play hero music. With exaggerated swimming movements, Aquaman goes and rescues Teresa. The family all gather round her, giving hugs.

Teresa:	Thank you! You saved my life and my shell.
Mrs Wood:	Yes, thank you so much.

Aquaman:	Not at all, ma'am! I'm Aquaman and this is my territory. You can trust me to be watching out for you at Beachquest. All in a day's work! *(Flexing his muscles)* I work out to the max so you can relax!
Auntie May:	A fellow poet. How marvellous!
Woody:	Wow! How cool is that!
All:	Woody, you can talk!
Woody:	Oops!

Play the theme music.

Reproduced with permission from *Let's Get Together!* by Sue Langwade (Barnabas for Children, 2013)

 www.barnabasinchurches.org.uk

Chip's Bible bloodhound challenge

At the end of each session, give out a sheet containing some 'Bible bloodhound' verses and suggestions for a family activity. The Bible verses are in some way connected to the session themes, as portrayed in the Wood family serial drama, and could serve to initiate some discussion at home. It would be helpful to make some Bibles available to borrow, for families who do not have their own at home.

Session One: The tree is planted

Theme: Belonging

Chip says: 'In the drama, the Wood family rescued me, gave me a new name—Chip, which suits me down to the ground—and took me home to belong to their family.'

Have a go at being a Bible bloodhound by looking up the following verses in a Bible and seeing if you can sniff out any connection between them and the drama.

- 1 John 3:1
- Luke 15:4–7
- 1 Peter 2:9–10

Chip's challenge

Have a go at making a sheep sock puppet and then try retelling the lost sheep story from the point of view of the sheep. What was his name? How did it feel to belong to the shepherd? Is there anyone you know who might be a 'lost sheep', feeling sad and lonely? Perhaps you could invite them over one day.

Session Two: The sapling tree

Theme: Appropriate boundaries and encouragement

Chip says: 'I hope you enjoyed my training session! The Wood family wanted me to learn to obey them, so that they could help me stay safe. They knew that a good way to train me would be to give me lots of encouragement in the form of my favourite treat—sausages. Teresa was very patient, wasn't she?'

Have a go at being a Bible bloodhound by looking up the following verses in a Bible and seeing if you can sniff out any connection between them and the drama.

- 1 Corinthians 13:4–7
- Psalm 119:165–168
- Proverbs 22:6
- Ephesians 6:1–4

Chip's challenge

Perhaps you could play a game you haven't tried before. Think about how the rules help you to play it properly: it's much easier when you are given clear rules. Chat about the rules you have in your household, remembering to let everyone have their say. You might like to have a go at making your own family Ten Commandments. Think about how patient God is when he is trying to teach us something new. How can you help each other learn new things?

Session Three: The tree bears fruit

Theme: Valuing ourselves and others

Chip says: 'The Wood family made me a fantastic kennel by all working together and doing their bit (even Auntie May!).'

Have a go at being a Bible bloodhound by looking up the following verses in a Bible and seeing if you can sniff out any connection between them and the drama.

- 1 Corinthians 12:14–20
- Ephesians 4:2–8
- Psalm 133:1–3

Chip's challenge

Do a jigsaw together (I recommend a doggy-themed one, of course), and chat about the different things you are each good at and how you could help each other. You could also make a habitat for some insects or hedgehogs, making sure everyone gets a chance to share their ideas, of course.

Session Four: The tree sends out seeds

Theme: Sharing what we have

Chip says: 'Wow! Wasn't it amazing that my old bone turned out to be something really useful? It wasn't much, but it was precious to me and I'm so glad I gave it up, because now we all get to stay together in the lovely Wood family home.'

Have a go at being a Bible bloodhound by looking up the following verses in a Bible and seeing if you can sniff out any connection between them and the drama.

- Matthew 13:31–33
- Luke 21:1–4
- Galatians 6:9–10

Chip's challenge

You could have a sort-out and bless someone else by taking some of your things to the charity shop. Collect up stray coins and start a collection for some people who don't have very much—remember, little things soon add up. Have a go at making some pizza dough and watch how a tiny bit of yeast makes the dough rise. Get your family or friends to add their favourite toppings and enjoy a pizza feast.

Session Five: The tree in maturity

Theme: Resting on God's promises

Chip says: 'Thank goodness Aquaman was watching out for Teresa! Something very serious might have happened to her if he hadn't come to her rescue. I'd better improve my doggy-paddle as soon as possible.'

Have a go at being a Bible bloodhound by looking up the following verses in a Bible and seeing if you can sniff out any connection between them and the drama.

- Psalm 121
- Proverbs 18:10
- Ephesians 1:18–23
- Jeremiah 17:7–8

Chip's challenge

Try going swimming together and make sure that everyone learns how to swim, so that you won't get into trouble like Teresa.

You could make a rainbow jelly using the recipe below and, as you eat it, remember that God promises to watch over us. Even though we sometimes get out of our depth, he will always be there to help us.

Buy a selection of different-coloured jellies (strawberry, orange, lemon, lime and blackcurrant), make them up according to the packet instructions and leave to stand at room temperature. Pour one jelly into a mould that is deep enough to accommodate all the layers. Put into the fridge until the jelly is just set and then add the next layer. Repeat until you have as many layers as you want.

If you want some 'creamy' layers, replace 125ml of the boiling water with 125ml of evaporated milk.

Interactive sketch

The purpose of this sketch is not only to have fun (though I hope you will), but to reinforce, in a very simple way, the overall theme of 'family' and the particular focus for each of the sessions. You can use the suggestions given for actions or invent your own. Either way, I'm sure it will be a unique creation as you will bring your own particular group dynamic to the piece.

If you are not doing all the sessions, select the verses that are relevant to you and repeat the chorus as many times as you like, perhaps varying the order of the 'Yo', 'Awesome' and so on. All should become clear as you read on.

Each session, teach everybody the actions, plus the chorus. (There are only four verses, allowing you to use the fifth session to put the whole piece together.) You will need to divide your group into four subgroups, each taking one of the words or phrases at the end of the chorus, which you will need to 'conduct'. (Don't worry, this just means that you point your finger at each of the groups in turn, maintaining a simple rhythm, and they shout out their given response as loudly and expressively as possible. Easy peasy!) If you want everyone to join in with the words as well as the actions, you will need to make sure words are available. Alternatively, you can organise 'live' readers, or the actions can be performed to a pre-recorded track. (See www.barnabasinchurches.org.uk/extra-resources/ for downloads.) You will need to judge what is best in your particular circumstances.

If you are including the piece in a service at a later date, quickly teach the congregation the actions for the chorus, which can all be done while sitting down, and divide them into four groups for the responses (Yo, Awesome, Amazing, Oh yeah!). Practise a couple of times until you think they have it.

Those who attended the sessions can then (either all together or in groups, depending on numbers) perform all the actions, encouraging the whole congregation to join in the chorus, with the 'conductor' directing proceedings. It would probably be helpful to have the words available on whatever visual system you use.

God joined us together

Chorus

God loves you and God loves me *(Point index finger at someone else, then thumb at self)*
He joined us in his family *(Link fingers of both hands together)*
Not one of us is the same *(Wag finger and shake head)*
But he knows us all by name! *(Pat yourself on the head)*
Young or old *(Suck thumb, and then adopt a walking stick pose)*
Big or small *(Stretch up high, then low)*
Our God loves us all! *(Hands over heart on top of each other, pulse)*
He does! *(Both thumbs up!)*
Yo! Awesome! Amazing! Oh yeah! *(Conductor conducts)*

Verse for Session One

You might say, what's in a name? *(Look around and shrug your shoulders)*
Won't a rose still smell the same *(Mime sniffing a rose)*
If it's called a pongeroo or weedywee? *(Make a disgusted face)*
But God's name holds so much treasure *(Mime holding something huge)*
It's impossible to measure *(Measure upwards in stages with your hand, stretching as high as possible)*
And he shares it all with you and li'l old me! *(Gesture towards others, then self)*

Use Chorus.

Verse for Session Two

You know God only gives us rules *(Mime unrolling a scroll, reading it and looking worried)*
To keep us safe from harm (how·cool!) *(In pairs, one stand in front of the other in a protective stance)*
And to free us to be who we really are! *(Mime letting a bird fly out of your hands)*
He's always there to cheer us on *(Wave both hands)*
'Cos he loves each and every one *(High-fives to others in group)*
And with Jesus we can reach up for the stars! *(Stretch up as far as you can)*

Use Chorus.

Verse for Session Three

Are you a lemon or a pear? (*Trace lemon then pear shape in the air*)
No one should feel they must compare (*Look each other up and down*)
Everyone has such a special part to play (*Mime passing something on from one to the other*)
So of your unique gifts make use (*Each mime something you're good at or you love to do*)
And let God squeeze out all your juice (*Give yourself a big squeeze*)
Then come back to him for filling every day. (*Lift hands to heaven*)

Use Chorus.

Verse for Session Four

Go on and spread your seeds abroad! (*Mime sowing seeds*)
What you've been given you shouldn't hoard (*Mime hanging on to something*)
Mul-ti-ply-ing is a heavenly decree (*Mexican wave*)
Trust God's Spirit to do the rest (*Point upwards*)
That's always better than the best (*Both thumbs up*)
Soon the angels will be giggling with glee! (*Mime giggling angels*)

Use Chorus.

Reflective prayer time

The reflective prayer time is, fairly obviously, a time for everyone to pause and think for a few moments about some of the things they have discovered throughout the session. This quieter, more thoughtful time also gives an opportunity for people to respond if they want to, either by participating in a simple action or by praying silently. A response should never be forced, just facilitated. Therefore, whoever is leading the prayer time needs to be sensitive, providing a calm, safe place for this to happen.

Depending on numbers, you may want to do the prayer time in small groups, allowing a greater sense of intimacy, or you may feel that people would benefit more from the anonymity of larger numbers. You will need to decide what you think best suits your situation. If you can accommodate it, sitting in a circle will help everyone to feel included and allows any visual aid to be placed centrally. Depending on the make-up of your group, you may want to have the visual aid on a table rather than on the floor.

It is probably best to keep the prayer time short enough to prevent younger participants from getting bored, but not so hurried that no one has time to think. Each time, ask if anyone would like to briefly share anything that they have discovered. Allow a short time for them to gather their thoughts. Then summarise the main points of the session, as outlined below, and use the suggested action or one of your own choosing, to reinforce what has been presented.

Session One: The tree is planted
Your name on the palm of God's hand

- We are planted with a purpose. We belong to God's family and he cares for each one.
- We have discovered some amazing things about God by thinking about his names.

Mention that the Bible tells us that God has our names written on the palm of his hand, because he loves us so much. Provide a large outline of the palm of a hand, a small card for each person and some pens. Invite people to write their name on the card, individually or as a family, and place it on the palm. As they do so, they should thank God for his love and provision for them and their family.

Session Two: The sapling tree

The two most important commandments

- God gives us boundaries and rules to help keep us safe.
- He also gives us lots of encouragement, and we can do that for one another too.

Remind everyone of the ten helpful rules that God gave the people of Israel. Say that the Bible tells us that Jesus summed them up into two really important rules:

- Love God with every part of you.
- Love others as much as you love yourself.

Bring a bowl of jelly babies—enough for each person to take two. Invite everyone to take two jelly babies and, as they eat them, to think first about loving God with their whole selves and second about loving others as much as they love themselves (friends, neighbours, people in your church and street, people overseas), and to say a special prayer for God to bless and encourage them. (If you would rather avoid using anything edible, use 'people' shapes cut out of craft foam or felt.)

Session Three: The tree bears fruit

Sharing fruit

- God loves variety and has made each one of us unique.
- We should celebrate who we are and appreciate others who are different from us.
- It can be fun learning to work together.

Bring a big bowl of fruit or fruit slices. Invite everyone to look at the different colours and shapes and to think about the different textures and flavours. Some may be tangy, some sweet and so on. Invite everyone to take a piece of fruit and, as they eat it, to thank God for the different sorts of people they know— some shy, some noisy, some young, some elderly—and to thank God that all are valuable to him. Be aware of health and safety, checking for allergies and that children are not likely to choke. Again, if you want an alternative, use a variety of seeds or flowers instead (not to eat, of course, just to look at).

Session Four: The tree sends out seeds

Stones and ripples

- We need to be willing to 'send out' what we have so that it can grow.
- We all have something to give.
- No matter how insignificant we may feel our offering is, God can do amazing things with it.

Mention that we may not always see the effect our giving has, but we trust God that he will use whatever we offer. Provide a basket of various sized stones and a container of water. Invite everyone to take a stone and place it in the water, watching the ripples it makes. As they do this, they could thank God that, with him, our giving can be multiplied and will go on having an effect even when we've forgotten about it.

Session Five: The tree in maturity

Rainbow promises

- We can trust God.
- He has made promises for our families and he will keep them.
- Even when times are difficult, he is watching over us.
- He has told us not to worry because he is on our side.

Using coloured paper, make a drawing or display of seven balloons, each in one of the colours of the rainbow. Each balloon should have a 'tail' of ribbon attached. Lay the display on the floor or the table. Have some sticky pads or glue available. On each balloon, write a promise God has made for us and our families.

Invite everyone to look at the rainbow colours and think about how God keeps his promises. The rainbow is a sign of this. Balloons remind us that we have lots to celebrate because we can trust God and know that he is always watching over us. Provide rainbow shapes cut out of paper. Invite everyone to take a rainbow and add it to the string attached to one of the balloons as a way of claiming the promises (saying, 'Yes, God, I agree with you').

Follow-up service

After the excitement of running a five-session programme, you'll probably be keen to plan a participatory, inclusive service to finish it off. This is a great way to include all those members of your congregation who have not been able to attend the sessions but want to feel part of what has happened. It is also an opportunity to introduce everyone to the overall theme of family and to use some of the elements from the various sessions, drawing others in to be a part of what has taken place, rather than just having them observe what they've missed.

As many of the elements can be shared with a wider audience (viewing the drama or puppet sketches, joining in with the interactive sketch or creating crafts, adding their own to those already produced, and even participating in a time of reflective prayer), it should not be too difficult for people to feel included. You will need to decide what fits best into your existing liturgy or, if you are able to hold a 'bespoke' service, how much you want to include. Also, choose which of the themes from the programme you think will be most suitable. It's probably best to use the elements relating to one of the themes, rather than confusing matters by changing the focus too often. Session One is probably the most suitable for people who are not familiar with the programme, as the message fits the situation—that is, that we belong to God and to each other and are all part of the same spiritual family (whether or not we belong to the same church).

You will, of course, need to set the elements in context and judge what will fit best with the character of your congregation. However, it should be easy enough to put together something that gives a flavour of what has happened, enabling those who weren't in attendance to get a 'taster' and to feel included. If you have space, it would be fantastic if you could set up a small craft area for people to visit as they enter, perhaps using the quick craft from Session One (putting your handprint on God's family tree). Display the original tree and invite others to add their own palm print.

If you think that paint might be too messy, either prepare some suitably coloured hand shapes, cut out in various sizes, or invite people to draw round their own hands and cut out the shape. People can then add their 'leaves' to the existing tree. If you don't have enough space for this, give a hand shape to all those who don't already feature on the tree, as they come into the building, explaining what it represents and inviting them to add themselves to the tree.

If at all possible, make tea, coffee and biscuits available before the service, so that people can chat about the programme and everyone can have a good mingle, while those who need to can catch up with the crafts. This can also provide a useful opportunity to make sure that any visitors are welcomed and made to feel drawn in before you've even started.

There are instructions included in the introduction to the interactive sketch, detailing how you might include it in a service. The most important thing is to have a 'conductor' who is confident in what they're doing. This is not something you can land on someone at the last minute. If you want to use favourite bits from each of the sessions, you will need to formulate a connective piece. The tree visual should help with this, facilitating a whistle-stop tour of the whole programme. As you might not want to repeat a reflective prayer idea, for the sake of those who were there first time, you could use the following idea, which is fairly 'all-purpose'.

Bring a watering can with a small amount of water in it, a container with soil in it, a light source, a bulb and a few seeds. Explain how, through the week, you have learnt that a healthy tree needs to be planted in good soil and have access to water, light and air. You are going to use those things to remind everyone of some of the gifts we have to thank God for. Ask for some volunteers, or prime some beforehand (perhaps a family), to help with the following reflection.

Plant the bulb in the container of soil… ask everyone to take a moment to silently thank God that we are safely planted in his family… Pour a little water on the bulb… ask everyone to silently thank God for Jesus, who washes away our sins and is the living water who refreshes us every day.

Light up the light source… ask everyone to thank God for the light of his word, which helps us to know the right way to go.

Plant the seeds in the soil and ask people to think of a person, a situation or a request that they would like to leave with God, like a seed awaiting the proper time to grow.

Thank God that we can leave our needs and desires in the soil of his presence, knowing that we can trust him to answer our prayers in the very best way.

Thank him for the Holy Spirit, the divine air that we breathe, who interprets all our requests to the Father as he reads our hearts so perfectly. Amen

Finally, it might be good to include a sharing time, allowing people to talk about their favourite part of the programme or to recount a funny event, building on the idea that telling our stories is an important way of keeping the ongoing 'Acts' alive.

Appendices

Silly laws quiz

Which of these is an existing law?

1. In Baltimore, Maryland, it is illegal to:

- Take a lion to the movies. (*True*)
- Stand on your left foot in public.
- Write letters on pink paper.

2. In the UK:

- Eating stewed beef on Christmas Day is banned.
- Eating mince pies on Christmas Day is banned. (*True*)
- Eating your own finger on Christmas Day is banned.

3. In Vermont:

- Women must obtain written permission from their husbands to wear false teeth. (*True*)
- Men must obtain written permission from their wives to wear false teeth.
- Dogs must have matching collars and leads.

4. It is illegal in Alabama to:

- Take a bath on a Monday.
- Wave to a friend using your left hand.
- Be blindfolded while driving a vehicle. (*True*)

5. In the UK, it is illegal to enter the Houses of Parliament wearing:

- A suit of armour. (*True*)
- Odd socks.
- A Manchester United shirt.

Here are some more bizarre rules and regulations, just for fun.

- It is illegal to die in the Houses of Parliament.
- It is an act of treason to place a postage stamp bearing the British king or queen's image upside down.
- In the UK, a pregnant woman can legally relieve herself anywhere she wants, including in a policeman's helmet.
- The head of any dead whale found on the British coast automatically becomes the property of the king, and the tail is the property of the queen.
- It is illegal not to tell the tax man anything you do not want him to know, but legal not to tell him information you do not mind him knowing.

HTTP://NEWS.BBC.CO.UK/1/HI/7081038.STM (CORRECT AT TIME OF PRINTING)

Names of God

- Elohim: The all-powerful one, the Creator (Genesis 1:1)
- Elyon: God most high (Genesis 14:18, 22)
- El Roi: The God who sees me (Genesis 16:13, 14)
- El Shaddai: God almighty, the all-sufficient one (Genesis 17:1)
- El Olam: The eternal or everlasting God (Genesis 21:33)
- Jehovah-Jireh: The Lord will provide (Genesis 22:14)
- Jehovah (YHWH): (I am), the self-existent one (Lord) (Exodus 3:14–15)
- Jehovah-Rapha: The Lord who heals (Exodus 15:26)
- Jehovah-Nissi: The Lord my banner (Exodus 17:15)
- Jehovah-Mekaddishkem: The Lord who sanctifies (Exodus 31:13)
- El Kanna, Esh Oklah: Jealous God, consuming fire (Exodus 34:14; Deuteronomy 4:24)
- Qedosh (Yisrael): The holy one (of Israel) (Leviticus 19:1–2)
- Jehovah-Shalom: The Lord is peace (Judges 6:24)
- Jehovah-Tsebaoth: The Lord of hosts (1 Samuel 17:45–46)
- Adonai: My great lord, my master (Psalm 16:2)
- Jehovah-Rohi: The Lord my shepherd (Psalm 23:1)
- Jehovah-Tsuri: The Lord my rock (Psalm 144:1)
- Jehovah-Tsidqenu: The Lord our righteousness (Jeremiah 23:6)

Reproduced with permission from *Let's Get Together!* by Sue Langwade (Barnabas for Children, 2013)
www.barnabasinchurches.org.uk

Word searches

Session One: The tree is planted

```
Y  Y  E  M  P  E  O  G  L  Z
V  R  O  O  T  Z  C  W  F  K
Z  M  W  U  Q  T  F  P  N  S
D  N  A  F  G  N  T  R  E  E
G  B  E  L  O  N  G  A  W  O
U  P  R  I  N  A  M  E  T  M
J  L  L  O  V  E  D  Y  L  Q
R  A  B  Z  J  B  M  I  N  E
S  N  T  O  G  E  T  H  E  R
U  T  F  P  O  S  S  E  S  S
```

name	root
loved	own
belong	tree
together	plant
possess	mine

Reproduced with permission from *Let's Get Together!* by Sue Langwade (Barnabas for Children, 2013)
www.barnabasinchurches.org.uk

Session Two: The sapling tree

```
S E J A I N W A L M
L A N S G L O V E D
P R F C E U X I W A
P P I E O C I N Q J
W R L G T U U D E N
R S A R H Y R R E S
O V L I U T N A E A
N A H Q S L N V G O
G R K Z F E E M D E
W A M D L A W L R L
```

loved	right
secure	rule
guide	praise
encourage	law
safety	wrong

Reproduced with permission from *Let's Get Together!* by Sue Langwade (Barnabas for Children, 2013)
www.barnabasinchurches.org.uk

Session Three: The tree bears fruit

```
R  G  C  V  U  D  X  P  G  V
S  N  T  O  A  W  M  E  H  K
M  L  I  H  N  L  G  A  J  P
Y  P  O  M  H  T  U  R  P  S
U  Z  O  R  T  A  E  E  M  E
W  W  Q  A  A  E  P  N  F  H
Z  H  M  X  E  N  A  P  T  B
H  O  S  E  E  D  G  M  Y  O
R  L  E  M  O  N  L  E  H  O
F  E  S  R  B  O  D  Y  I  N
```

whole	body
seed	team
lemon	content
orange	happy
pear	me

Reproduced with permission from *Let's Get Together!* by Sue Langwade (Barnabas for Children, 2013)

www.barnabasinchurches.org.uk

Session Four: The tree sends out seeds

```
M  H  L  T  I  P  L  Y  X  L
I  U  E  M  E  N  T  O  R  E
R  Y  L  B  L  E  S  S  T  A
A  P  O  T  M  O  D  E  L  R
C  K  T  P  I  V  W  S  O  N
L  D  S  L  I  P  T  L• E  G
E  K  L  I  T  T  L  E  L  R
M  L  T  B  K  X  R  Y  N  P
D  Q  S  P  G  I  V  I  N  G
S  M  I  L  E  W  L  R  C  Z
```

learn	mentor
bless	model
multiply	miracle
lots	giving
little	smile

Reproduced with permission from *Let's Get Together!* by Sue Langwade (Barnabas for Children, 2013)
www.barnabasinchurches.org.uk

Session Five: The tree in maturity

```
F  A  I  T  H  F  U  L  Q  H
S  L  P  G  T  E  N  J  O  Y
J  S  O  L  E  R  K  V  V  E
E  T  R  V  F  U  U  R  O  D
F  O  M  A  E  A  J  S  Y  E
R  R  P  N  I  D  T  K  T  I
E  M  A  S  K  N  Q  H  L  U
L  S  R  B  A  G  B  I  E  X
A  L  T  O  O  N  A  O  R  R
X  U  Y  A  R  M  S  J  W  Z
```

faithful	rainbow
enjoy	storms
trust	arms
father	relax
loved	party

Reproduced with permission from *Let's Get Together!* by Sue Langwade (Barnabas for Children, 2013)

www.barnabasinchurches.org.uk

Serial drama extra scene

Episode three: To the dog house

When 'Voice off' has finished, Auntie May enters.

Auntie May: Hello, everyone! I'm Auntie May de Wood. I'm a very good poet, you know, and I just can't help myself writing wonderful poetry to mark special occasions. Well, this is a very special occasion. We've adopted a marvellous dog called Chip and today we're building him a brand new kennel. I've written a couple of poems to mark this event, so do you mind if I share them with you? You can tell me which one you think will be best.

There once was a doggy with no place to call his own
So the Wood family came and took him to their home.
'Woof, Woof,' he cried, as they called out his name.
He'd never have to sleep in a lonely place again! *(Sobs)*

Or how about:

There once was a doggy called Chip,
Who was so sad, he started to yip!
Yip, yippy, yip, yip,
I'm an unhappy Chip,
And his tears fell down in a big drip!

Noises off.

Auntie May: Oh, they're all coming now. We'd better decide later!

Rockin' person award

Cut out the shapes and glue the top halves together, ensuring that the print is facing outwards. Spread the lower halves outwards and watch your figure rock!

Box net

Cut out along the bold lines. Fold along the dotted lines. Put glue on the parts that are shaded in.

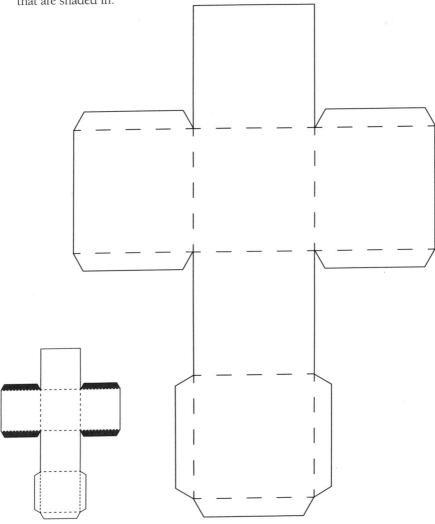

Reproduced with permission from *Let's Get Together!* by Sue Langwade (Barnabas for Children, 2013)
www.barnabasinchurches.org.uk
132

Bread and fish paper chain template

Cut along the bold lines. Fold in a concertina fashion. Cut around the shape, being careful not to cut the folded edge.

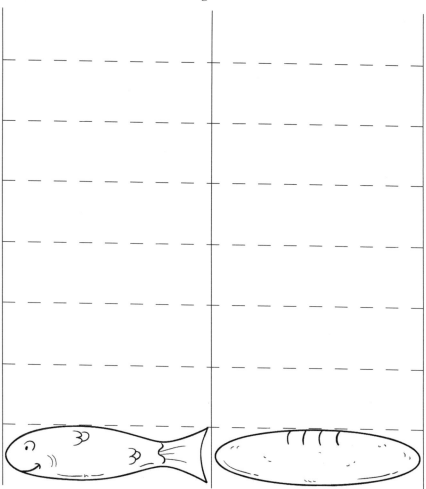

Reproduced with permission from *Let's Get Together!* by Sue Langwade (Barnabas for Children, 2013)

 www.barnabasinchurches.org.uk

Colouring activity

Session One: The tree is planted
Theme: Belonging

Colour in the pictures and then draw a line to join up the pairs that belong together.

Reproduced with permission from *Let's Get Together!* by Sue Langwade (Barnabas for Children, 2013)
www.barnabasinchurches.org.uk

Colouring activity

Session Two: The sapling tree
Theme: Appropriate boundaries and encouragement

Colour in the pictures, and later you can cut them out and stick them on to card. Make them into badges by taping a safety-pin to the back. Encourage someone by giving them a badge to wear.

Reproduced with permission from *Let's Get Together!* by Sue Langwade (Barnabas for Children, 2013)

www.barnabasinchurches.org.uk

Colouring activity

Session Three: The tree bears fruit

Theme: Valuing ourselves and others

Colour in the picture, then cut out the pieces carefully and see if someone in your family can put them together again.

Reproduced with permission from *Let's Get Together!* by Sue Langwade (Barnabas for Children, 2013)
www.barnabasinchurches.org.uk

Colouring activity

Session Four: The tree sends out seeds
Theme: Sharing what we have

When we bless others, we help God's kingdom to grow.

Reproduced with permission from *Let's Get Together!* by Sue Langwade (Barnabas for Children, 2013)
www.barnabasinchurches.org.uk

Colouring activity

Session Five: The tree in maturity
Theme: Resting on God's promises

Colour in the border and the rainbow, then punch holes where the black dots are. Thread some wool through the holes and you can hang up your picture to remind you that God always keeps his promises.

Reproduced with permission from *Let's Get Together!* by Sue Langwade (Barnabas for Children, 2013)
www.barnabasinchurches.org.uk

Few Children, Great Opportunities

12 stand-alone sessions for mixed-age church-based groups

Sue Price and Ruth Alliston

Few Children, Great Opportunities contains twelve ready-to-use thematic sessions exploring the character of God through the model we see in Jesus. The programme is ideal for church-based children's work where there are small numbers of children and an age range from 3 to 11 years. Because a small number of children with a mixed age range also defines many families, the material can be adapted for home use by families who want to spend time growing in faith together.

The sessions can be used in any order while building on each other. The material seeks to engage head, heart and hands by giving several ways to tell a Bible story using different learning styles, offering a variety of activities that help children to engage with the story, and including original songs, rhymes and chants as well as non-musical ways to worship God.

The twelve characteristics of God explored in the programme include love, faithfulness, patience, power, goodness, self-control, peace, trustworthiness, kindness, gentleness and joy.

ISBN 978 1 84101 880 5   £8.99

Available from your local Christian bookshop or, in case of difficulty, direct from BRF: please visit www.barnabasforchurches.org.uk

Also from BRF/Barnabas

Fill the Gap!

120 instant Bible games for Sunday schools and midweek groups

Rebecca Parkinson

Fill the Gap! contains 120 easy-to-play Bible-based games with little or no preparation needed—perfect for picking straight off the shelf. The ideas are designed to help local churches fill up those awkward gaps of time in Sunday schools, midweek clubs, holiday clubs, after-school clubs and children's camps.

The games are divided equally across the Old Testament and the New Testament and offer a fun-filled way to reinforce a teaching point or help children who are unfamiliar with Bible stories. There are two games for each story, one aimed at 4–7s and the other at 7–11s, but many of the games can be modified slightly to make them appropriate for older or younger children to take part.

Most of the games are suitable for both smaller and larger groups of children and many can be easily adapted to fit different Bible stories, allowing favourite games to be used again with a different emphasis.

ISBN 978 0 85746 004 2   £8.99

Available from your local Christian bookshop or, in case of difficulty, direct from BRF: please visit www.barnabasforchurches.org.uk

Paper Plate Bible Crafts

58 easy-to-do ideas for 5–7s

Anita Reith Stohs

Paper Plate Bible Crafts is a great resource for fun crafts that teach favourite Bible stories in any setting.

Fast, inexpensive and readily available, paper plates easily become masks, mobiles, puppets and plaques. The finished crafts are an ingenious way to reinforce Bible stories and themes.

The book includes 58 tried and tested ideas for 5–7s, each with simple templates and easy-to-follow instructions. Alongside the paper plate, each craft uses basic, everyday materials such as card, felt-tipped pens, scissors and glue and can be completed as suggested or adapted to suit the needs and skills of the children.

Each craft idea includes:

- Key Bible story reference
- Full equipment list
- Easy-to-follow instructions
- Simple discussion starters
- Alternative ideas for making the craft
- Illustration of the finished craft

ISBN 978 0 85746 261 9   £7.99

Available from your local Christian bookshop or, in case of difficulty, direct from BRF: please visit www.brfonline.org.uk

Starting Your Messy Church

A beginner's guide for churches

Lucy Moore and Jane Leadbetter

If you're wondering about starting a Messy Church®, this book is for you. It's short, punchy and easily passed round a team who may not have time to read the longer Messy Church books or watch the DVD. It gets the basics across quickly and will give you a good idea of whether or not Messy Church is for you. It sets out clearly just what you'll need to consider and will also help you avoid some of the pitfalls that other teams have encountered on their Messy Church journeys.

Topics covered include:

- What Messy Church is and isn't
- Why the values?
- Commitment needed
- Checklist of starting strategies
- Organising your team
- Sustaining your Messy Church

Sales of this book help fund BRF's Messy Church® ministry

ISBN 978 0 85746 050 9   £4.99

Available from your local Christian bookshop or, in case of difficulty, direct from BRF: please visit www.barnabasforchurches.org.uk

Enjoyed
this book?

Write a review—we'd love to hear what you think.
Email: reviews@brf.org.uk

Keep up to date—receive details of our new books as they happen.
Sign up for email news and select your interest groups at:
www.brfonline.org.uk/findoutmore/

Follow us on Twitter @brfonline

By post—to receive new title information by post (UK only), complete
the form below and post to: BRF Mailing Lists, 15 The Chambers, Vineyard,
Abingdon, Oxfordshire, OX14 3FE

Your Details
Name _____
Address_____
_____
Town/City _____ Post Code _____
Email_____

Your Interest Groups (*Please tick as appropriate)

☐ Advent/Lent	☐ Messy Church
☐ Bible Reading & Study	☐ Pastoral
☐ Children's Books	☐ Prayer & Spirituality
☐ Discipleship	☐ Resources for Children's Church
☐ Leadership	☐ Resources for Schools

Support your local bookshop
Ask about their new title information schemes.